MICROSOFT DYNAMICS GP

SECURITY AND AUDIT FIELD MANUAL

Mark Polino,CPA.CFF.CITP
Andy Snook,CRISC

Dynamics GP 2016

First published: September 2017

Published by:

Fastpath, Inc.
4093 NW Urbandale Drive
Des Moines, IA
www.gofastpath.com

Book Layout © 2014 BookDesignTemplates.com

Microsoft Dynamics GP Security and Audit Field Manual / Mark Polino, Andy Snook. --
1st ed., Dynamics GP 2016

ISBN-13: 978-1975981846
ISBN-10: 1975981847

CREDITS

Authors
Mark Polino
Andy Snook

Editor
Ann Deiterich
Gina McGlamry

Reviewers
Belinda Allen
Gina McGlamry

Project Coordinator
Trish Boccuti

Cover
Phoenix 3 Marketing

Production Assistant
John Tuttle

ABOUT THE AUTHORS

Mark Polino is a Certified Public Accountant (CPA) with additional certifications in information technology (CITP) and financial forensics (CFF). His work has centered around Dynamics GP for more than 18 years. Mark is a ten-year Microsoft MVP. He has been recognized as a GPUG All Star, and he is an Advanced Credentialed Professional for Dynamics GP. Mark is the author or coauthor of seven other Dynamics GP-focused books, along with two novels. He runs the popular DynamicAccounting.net website and writes a regular column for MS Dynamics world. He frequently speaks on Dynamics GP topics. Mark can be found on Twitter at @mpolino.

Andy Snook is certified in Risk and Information Systems Controls (CRISC) as well as certified in Microsoft Dynamics and SAP. He is an active member of the Dynamics User Groups (GPUG, AXUG, NAVUG, and CRMUG).

He has been designing audit and compliance solutions for over 15 years and has assisted with compliance projects at more than 100 companies. Under his leadership, Fastpath has grown to support more than 1,000 companies in over 30 different countries. Andy is a speaker at many industry events, the User Group Summit, Convergence, and GRC day.

Prior to his time at Fastpath, Andy was a financial systems implementation consultant for Microsoft Dynamics and an SAP management consultant with Ernst & Young. He graduated from the University of Notre Dame with degrees in Economics and Computer Applications. Andy tweets at @snookgofast.

ACKNOWLEDGMENTS

Mark Polino:

Andy Snook and I have talked about doing a book together for years and it's finally done. Thanks, Andy for making this a reality.

Thanks to Jeff Soelberg and Liz Piteo. This book wouldn't have been possible without your help, proving again that I don't know half as much as I think I do.

Thanks to Richard Whaley for pioneering the way for Dynamics GP books. **The Dynamics GP Security Handbook,** *now out of print, was the go to GP security book for many years. My hope is that this book can fill that need and more.*

Trish Boccuti, thanks for just making things happen like you always do.

Finally, a huge thanks to my wonderful wife Dara for putting up with all my book projects.

Andy Snook:

I would like to thank all the customers who have trusted me with their problems over the years. Without that trust, I wouldn't have the expertise I share within this book.

Thanks to Jeff Soelberg who showed me the value in completing v.1, and to Mike Cassady for keeping me honest. To the rest of my

Fastpath family, a guy couldn't ask for a better group of problem solvers.

To Mark Polino, thanks for finally turning this into a reality after years of my idle threats.

Finally, thanks to my parents who taught me the importance of learning, to Drew and Graham who taught me the importance of teaching, and to Katie, well, there isn't enough ink and paper.

CONTENTS

CONVENTIONS

In this book, we include a number of styles of text that distinguish different kinds of information. Here are the examples of these styles and an explanation of their meaning.

 Key foundational principles for a section are indicated with a tent. Principles serve as the basecamp for security design, setup, and monitoring.

 Warnings or important notes appear with the campfire symbol. Pay attention and don't get burned.

 Tips and tricks appear with a backpack symbol. Hang on to them to make life easier.

 Tools to make a process easier or more secure, are marked with the shovel icon. Tools can be free or paid.

The > symbol and included text indicates a cascade of menu items. For example, **File>Save** would direct the user to click on the **File** menu and then select **Save** from the menu dropdown.

New terms and **important words** are shown in bold.

FOREWORD

Business application controls are essential to the daily operations of the enterprise. Well implemented, they can prevent malicious use of data, while ensuring fidelity of information presented to stakeholders, shareholders, and business managers. The opposite can spell disaster and open the doors to costly mistakes, expensive lawsuits, or threaten business continuity. However, the task of setting up proper controls can be daunting, with emphasis usually placed on securing a few windows and reports, rather than enforcing business operational rules.

This book is designed, chapter after chapter, to explain good security and control principles, while offering clear guidance on how to implement these within Microsoft Dynamics GP. Fastpath uniquely blends its industry leadership in enterprise resource planning, audit, and compliance with its deep knowledge of Microsoft Dynamics GP and offers a "first-in-its-kind" book that is sure to put your organization on the right track of satisfying adequate user access to the application, with your need for sound security principles and controls.

Mariano Gomez Bent
Microsoft MVP
September 7, 2017
Atlanta, GA

{0}

INTRODUCTION

Enterprise Resource Planning (ERP) systems are the foundation of modern financial management. Gartner[1] is generally credited with coining the term in 1990's and today's ERP systems represent accounting and financial management applications used by organizations around the world. ERP systems manage trillions of dollars and contain untold amounts of critical corporate information. Yet, every day seems to bring a new story of corporate fraud, theft, or manipulation. All too often the dreaded words "a weakness in internal controls" appear as the cause.

This is a book about ERP security written to help users avoid becoming a victim of those dreaded words. Audit-focused books provide the theories to good security without addressing individual products. ERP-specific books narrowly address how to activate security features, but don't cover why a setting is important to the larger security picture. Indeed, ERP-focused texts often ignore the larger security picture that exists beyond application security settings.

Our goal is to combine theory and application elements into a book with the principles of good security applied to a specific ERP system. In each section, we'll address key security and audit principles, apply

---

[1] "Extended ERP reborn in b-to-b," Heather Herald: InfoWorld, August 27–September 3, 2001.

those to Dynamics GP, and cover specific steps for designing, setting, and validating security.

We want this book to be the resource that people look to for application security in Dynamics GP. For that reason, we've chosen a field manual approach for the look and feel of this book.

We expect that readers will have at least some knowledge of application security and at least basic navigation knowledge of Dynamics GP.

{1}

SECURITY PRINCIPLES

Purpose of Security

Why have security in ERP systems at all? Doesn't information want to be free? Certainly, information is a remarkable escape artist, but Information has value and ensuring the accuracy of information is important to validating financial statements and their underlying transactions. In short, it comes down to trust.

The information in an ERP system documents and describes financial transactions. We must be able to trust this documentation to accurately reflect the actual transaction. We also need to be able to trust that transactions were properly authorized and executed as recorded. Without being overly dramatic, the core of our financial system rests on our ability to trust financial representations made by organizations. This reliance on company financial reports leads us to Ronald Reagan's well-known quote based on a Russian proverb, "Trust, but verify."[2]

In business, we trust that any given transaction works as expected when it's processed. Individually verifying every transaction as it occurs, is unreasonably expensive. Instead we implement security,

---

[2] Obront, "Doveryai, No Proveryai – Trust but verify", https://obront.wordpress.com/2011/06/06/doveryai-no-proveryai-trust-but-verify/

compliance, and control processes. Then we audit them to provide a level of assurance that they are working appropriately.

Security always requires a balance. Like a safe with no access doors, perfect security protects information from everyone, rendering the information useless in the process. Good security, compliance, and control processes are an ever-changing balancing act. Notice that in this description we don't rely on security alone. Security, compliance, and control processes work together to create layers of protection designed to compensate for potential failures. Failure in one area may be offset by a control in another section. For this reason, we've titled our six key principles for ERP security our Security Tent.

The Security Tent

Our Security Tent is made up of five poles and a surrounding canvas. The five poles are:

1. Access Review and Certification
2. Role Management
3. User Provisioning
4. Emergency Access Management
5. Monitoring

Our tent is then covered by:
6. Segregation of Duties/Risk Assessment

 The Security Tent represents the core principles on which we'll base security going forward. Let's take a quick look at our tent poles.

Access Review and Certification ensures that the access granted to users is being reviewed consistently on a predetermined basis to validate that users have appropriate security access. To certify that reviews are being performed, evidence of reviews needs to be retained.

Role Management looks at the design of security roles to reduce segregation of duties conflicts and improve security administration. Managing security via roles, instead of individual user permissions, reduces the number of control points and simplifies auditing. A well-designed set of roles can be key to improving both security and security management.

User Provisioning is the process used to create new users, including the process to request and approve access. User provisioning should generally include an approval workflow, either physical or electronic, to support the creation of new users.

Emergency Access Management is a function of both Role Management and User Provisioning designed to provide users with temporary access to elevated privileges. Emergency Access Management should include approval, monitoring, and follow up to ensure that emergency access is removed when it is no longer required. For example, if an accounting supervisor is out on a maternity leave, the person filling in may temporarily need the same level of access as the accounting supervisor. The critical word is "temporary". There must be a mechanism to remove access when the accounting supervisor returns.

Monitoring is the ability to observe transaction activities in the system to detect segregation of duties failures and respond accordingly.

These are the poles that hold up our security tent. The canvas that ties everything together is Segregation of Duties and the associated assessment of risk.

Segregation of Duties

Segregation of Duties (SoD) is a basic internal control that attempts to ensure that no single individual has the authority to execute two or more conflicting, sensitive transactions with the potential to impact financial statements. Responsibilities should be adequately spread out or segregated among multiple users. For example, allowing a user to both create and pay a vendor creates a risk of fraudulent payments designed to benefit that user. Segregation of duties would seek to reduce this risk by assigning responsibility for each task to a different user.

A key part of segregation of duties is risk assessment and management. The complete removal of all risk is irrational, and perfect segregation of duties, even if possible, would be inherently inefficient. The goal of our security tent is not to eliminate risk, but to provide a reasonable assessment of expected risks and take measures to manage, and mitigate, those risks.

People subconsciously evaluate risks all the time. Driving a car increases the risk of being injured or killed in a car accident. Hiding in the basement and not driving would radically reduce that risk, while making life more boring. The benefits of driving typically outweigh the risks. Instead of hiding under the bed, we accept the risks and seek to reduce them with safer car designs, airbags, seat belts, driving sober, etc. Insurance doesn't reduce the risk of an accident, but it mitigates the risk of financial loss. This type of risk-based approach also works well for ERP security.

As global accounting firm EY notes in "A Risk-Based Approach to Segregation of Duties"[3]:

Ultimately, it is critical for the company to understand and assess the landscape of current conflicts, reduce them to the extent possible for a given staffing model (via remediation initiatives) and apply mitigating controls to the remaining issues. This approach does not yield zero SoD conflicts, but demonstrates that management has evaluated existing conflicts and reduced residual risk to an acceptable level through tested and controlled processes. Typically, this solution is palatable to auditors, regulators and financial reporting stakeholders alike, and promotes the awareness of risk beyond a compliance-only exercise.

Risk-Based Approach

With a risk-based approach to ERP security, high risk items are addressed first, often with additional controls, increased segregation of duties, and greater scrutiny. The idea is to address the greatest risks

---

[3] EY, "A Risk-Based Approach to Segregation of Duties" Insights on Governance, Risk and Compliance (May 2010) http://www.ey.com/Publication/vwLUAssets/EY_Segregation_of_dutie s/$FILE/EY_Segregation_of_duties.pdf

first and with the most effort. That doesn't mean that lower risks are ignored; they just don't require the same level of controls and may be addressed later in the process.

Controls

Just as all risks are not created equal, all controls are not the same either. Controls generally fall into two major categories:

- Preventative Controls
- Detective Controls

Preventative Controls are designed to keep unauthorized activities and errors from occurring. For example, appropriate role management seeks to prevent users within an ERP system from accessing features to which they have been denied permission. If a user doesn't have permission to create a check, the ERP system should prevent that user from printing a check. Preventative controls are generally preferred over detective controls, but not exclusively. If unauthorized activities or errors can be prevented, that is usually the preferred choice.

Some examples of preventative controls include:

- Segregation of Duties
- Approvals
- Authorizations
- Verifications
- Physical control of assets

Detective Controls are designed to identify unauthorized activities and errors that *have* occurred. If a user is given improper access to refund a payment, for example, a regularly scheduled review of access permission might identify the problem so that the user's access could be changed. It would not prevent the problem, but it would identify it for later correction.

Users may also see references to **Reactive Controls**. Reactive controls are designed to limit any damage from a control failure. These are the fix, or the reaction, to a detective control. Essentially, this turns the result of a detective control into a preventative control. We've included reactive controls as a subset of detective controls.

Some examples of detective controls include:

- Reviews of Performance/Analytics
- Reconciliations
- Audits
- Physical counts (Inventory, Assets, etc.)

Even though segregation of duties is a preventative control, it overlaps the entire environment in the sense that users involved in detective controls shouldn't also be involved in the related transactions. That's why we refer to segregation of duties as the fabric covering our security tent. For example, a user with permission to deposit cash shouldn't be part of the detective control of reconciling the related bank account.

Controls can also be **Automatic** or **Manual**. For our purposes, automatic controls (system controls) represent controls present and activated in the ERP system. For example, validating that debits equal credits before allowing posting of a journal entry is a typical automatic control. Most ERP systems prevent users from posting an unbalanced journal entry automatically. Sometimes, automatic controls need to be activated. For example, requiring approval of journal entries may be a common automatic control, but often there are setup requirements for this control to become active. If appropriate setup hasn't been completed, this feature isn't functioning as a control, even though it exists.

Manual controls are controls that occur outside of the system. For instance, requiring a manual review and physical signature on a printed journal entry prior to entering the data into the system is a manual control. Theoretically, it is preventative and designed to provide greater control of journal entries. Since this control manually resides outside the system, only a detective control, like a review or journal entry matching process, can validate that the preventative control is working.

Detective controls are often manual as they frequently involve a user reviewing or analyzing information. Auditors typically require some type of evidence that a manual control is being applied before relying on it. This evidence is often a contemporaneous electronic or physical signature indicating that the control activity was performed.

Finally, it's important to have a mix of controls. Automatic, preventative controls are generally preferred because they offer protection that should be hard to manipulate. With an automatic, preventative control, software prevents users from performing operations not explicitly assigned to them. An automatic detective control, like an alert that generates when a user posts their own transaction, is a helpful check on the validity of preventative controls. However, an automatic detective control only works if a manual detective control is performed to review and evaluate the information generated. In our example, a review of the alert, with evidence that the review was performed to determine if that posting was appropriate, would provide a detective control.

Manual detective controls are also important for ensuring that any manual preventative controls are being performed. This includes items like reviewing transactions for proper sign-off.

Having a single set of controls is too rigid. If those controls fail, there is nothing left to catch errors, misstatements, or fraud. A mix of control types provides a depth of defensive layers to reduce risk.

A risk-based strategy should view controls as filters where appropriate information flows through the filter while errors, misstatements, and fraud are filtered out. Picture a layered water filter where each layer subsequently filters out smaller and smaller particles until what gets through is considered clean enough to drink. It's not perfectly distilled H_2O, extremely small particles will still get through, but the water won't make people sick. Similarly, in a well-designed control environment, financial transactions may still have issues, but the issues won't be large enough to harm the business.

Mitigation

Not all conflicts can be addressed with controls inside of an ERP system. As we've discussed with manual controls, a control process may need to exist outside of the system to properly address certain risks. Also, as we've mentioned, not all conflicts can be eliminated.

Mitigation doesn't prevent or correct a conflict, instead it allows the conflict to exist and creates or identifies controls that compensate for the risk associated with the conflict. Mitigation is the acceptance of risk associated with a conflict buffered by another control. **Mitigating controls** may also be referred to as compensating controls.

For example, in a small accounts payable department, a user who enters vouchers may also be able to change vendor addresses creating a risk of delivering of a valid check to a fraudulent address. A mitigating control would require that vendor address changes be reviewed monthly against the evidence for an address change, like a vendor notice. The mitigating control might not prevent an initial fraud, but it should limit the damage by identifying the improper change in a reasonable time.

Conflict Matrix

Ultimately, to get control of potential conflicts, a firm is going to need a **conflict matrix** that identifies potential conflicts, classifies the level of risk (like high, medium, and low), and identifies mitigating controls for items that can't be addressed in other ways. This is needed to set application security and identify gaps that need to be addressed. We'll deal with this more later as we get into design, but this is an important piece so don't skip it and jump right into setting up security.

Application

All of this is important when designing security for an ERP system. No system has a perfect set of automated controls and it is important to not underestimate the creativity, intentionally or unintentionally, of system users. The point of this section is to get users thinking about good internal controls as we work on the design of security for Dynamics GP. Keep in mind that there may be more than one way to provide the appropriate level of control, even if that requires a detective control or mitigation.

{2}

SECURITY DESIGN

- Access Review and Certification
- Role Management
- User Provisioning

Here, in Chapter 2, is where all the hard work around security is really done, in the design. In this chapter, we'll look at designing good security roles and provide an overview of how GP security is structured. This is a key part of role management and understanding what permissions a role provides. It's also an important part of user provisioning, specifically, understanding which roles should be assigned to various users. Finally, access review and certification involves validating that security is properly assigned. This makes understanding the security design critical to reviewing and certifying access.

Principles

Security Design

Good security is intentionally designed. It doesn't happen by accident. Too often companies simply rely on default security options and try to fit their user settings and processes into the defaults. This choice almost never provides appropriate security and segregation of duties. Instead, companies must do the hard work of designing security for the company's specific needs.

Designing security starts with understanding and mapping the organization's processes. A good security design includes identifying processes that are in scope, documenting those business processes, and then mapping them to the ERP system. Once the processes are mapped to the software, controls can be identified, both system and manual, to help design appropriate security.

The point of **process mapping** is to provide a holistic view of a specific process. This makes it more likely that companies will find holes, workarounds, and unknowns in a process that needs to be fixed. Process mapping also helps ensure that items are not overlooked when designing security, and it provides a bird's eye view to help identify segregation of duties issues. The full scope of process mapping is too big for this book, but there are lots of resources out there to help with the process.

It's important to work with multiple stakeholders when identifying processes in scope. Stakeholders can include individuals from accounting, finance, operations, IT, auditing or any other area affected by a specific process. Often the mapping is for a full process, like quote to cash, but depending on the systems involved, the scope may be reduced.

Involving auditors in the process of scoping and mapping processes is critically important.

Process Mapping

Once the scope has been determined, a useful tool for process mapping is a flowchart using swim lanes. In this tool, process flows are documented on the row belonging to their assigned role making it easy to identify where the responsibility belongs.

Responsible roles, departments, or positions appear in rows on the left. Processes flow from left to right and are shown in the associated responsibility row.

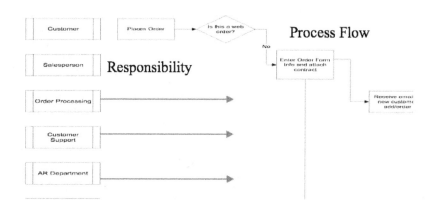

The method visually represents a process making it easy to understand. Process flows provide an opportunity to visually identify potential segregation of duties conflicts and control points. This is an area where comparing the process map to a conflict matrix helps find SoD conflicts for process corrections.

A conflict matrix would identify specific activities which create a conflict. Generically, this would be something like access to create vendors and generate checks. Specifically, this might be access to the Vendor Maintenance and Select Checks windows in Dynamics GP. A user with this access creates a risk of generating a check to a falsified vendor. Auditing firms can provide generic conflict matrices, but applying them to specific ERP applications can prove challenging.

Controls

Not all controls can be contained in application security. A good control environment contains a mix of controls including both automated and manual controls. Where security alone can't provide appropriate segregation of duties, other options, like workflow and scripting, can help fill the gap. Finally, mitigating controls including audit trails, reviews, and approvals are an important piece of the control environment.

After processes have been designed and diagrammed, they should be mapped to security roles. This mapping should be based on the operations being performed, not necessarily the user's title or job description. Using default roles is not recommended. Default roles were designed to allow users to perform a complete process. They weren't designed with appropriate segregation of duties in mind. Additionally, each company's situation is unique, and default roles simply won't appropriately address any given company's needs. A leading practice is to map processes to new custom roles.

Roles

In Dynamics GP, roles are the primary logical control. Mapping processes to roles ties security design to the application. In GP, users can belong to more than one role, and security for all assigned roles is active at the same time. This makes it important to consider all the roles that a user belongs to, and the underlying permissions, when reviewing appropriate segregation of duties.

Dynamics GP's standard roles can be changed. However, changing roles is not recommended because incorrectly removing a security operation may make it hard to revert to a working security role. For companies that choose to modify default roles, copying, renaming, and customizing a role is preferred. Custom roles don't have to be built from scratch, but building new roles using default tasks as the base is a leading practice for setting GP security. Default roles in Dynamics GP can be inactivated to prevent users from being assigned a standard role.

When designing roles, segregation of duties should be a key consideration. Roles that have inherent segregation of duties conflicts automatically create problems when they are assigned to a user, and inherent SoD conflicts should be avoided wherever reasonable.

For example, a role that allows a user to create bank transactions and reconcile the bank account is an inherent conflict that could allow a user to make and hide fraudulent transactions. Separating these two actions into different roles removes the inherent conflict. Users may still end up with conflicts when assigned to more than one role, but building roles with minimal conflicts at least eliminates inherent conflicts when assigning a given role.

Finally, GP offers additional security options that can be used to mitigate areas where role and task based security is inefficient and provide additional security depth.

Application

When designing security in Dynamics GP, it's important to understand some GP security specifics. In this section, we'll dig deeper into some GP security details to help the design process. In future chapters, we'll go into these items with more detail, specifically how to set them up.

Perimeter Security

Since Dynamics GP is primarily an on-premise ERP solution, perimeter security is the responsibility of the company running GP. This can include something like properly securing the network that provides access to Dynamics GP and the servers holding Dynamics GP data. A basic, and certainly not comprehensive, list would include:

- Properly securing the server operating system on the machine running Dynamics GP.
- Using strong network passwords and appropriate password policies including a lockout policy for incorrect passwords.
- Providing appropriate, limited network access.
- Use of an external firewall.
- Use of Virus protection.
- Properly securing SQL Server.
- Tightly controlling 'sa' access.

Most of these items are beyond the scope of this book and delve deeper into organizational IT security. Microsoft's Dynamics GP manual *Planning for Security* provides additional depth and recommendations on this topic. It's available as a free download at **https://www.microsoft.com/en-us/download/details.aspx?id=34666**.

One note, *Planning for Security* makes some generic recommendations, including the use of single sign on, that are not available for Dynamics GP natively. The only way to get single sign on for the Dynamics GP on-premise client is with the use of Config AD from Fastpath.

Dynamics GP creates SQL server users as part of its security setup for on premise users. Web client-only users can be setup to access GP using an Active Directory (AD) login, but their activity is limited to the web client. With GP on premise security, client passwords are transformed and encrypted preventing GP users from accessing SQL server directly. We cover this in more detail in Chapter 3 and it's also covered in the *Planning for Security* manual described above.

Types of Users

Before designing security, it's important to have at least a basic understanding of how security works in Dynamics. Here we'll look at how GP security works as part of our security design consideration. When designing Microsoft Dynamics GP security, there are three possible types of user licenses with varying costs and capabilities. They are:

- **Full Users** – Concurrent user license with full read/write access to Dynamics GP and limited only by security settings. This is the most expensive GP license.

- **Limited Users** – Concurrent user license where users can view (read) all information in Dynamics GP, but can only enter information related to their user. Essentially these are concurrent users with all the rights of self-serve users and additional view access. These users' access can be further limited by GP security and there are specific roles included for limited users.

- **Self-Serve Users** – Named user licenses where users can see and enter information for their own user only. This can be further limited by GP security. Self-Serve user licenses are the least expensive licensing option for Dynamics GP. With appropriate permission, self-serve users can enter or access these items for their user:

  - Purchase Requisition

  - Payroll Time card

  - Project Time sheet

  - Home Page Parts

  - Employee Profile

  - Paystubs

  - W4

  - Benefits

  - Direct Deposit

- Skills and Training

- Project Expense

- W2

Dynamics GP provides an inquiry window and a report to show users and assigned user types.

Roles and Tasks Overview

After processes have been designed and reviewed, they should be mapped to roles. In GP, a role is a set of tasks. Tasks are made up of security operations. Security operations are collected into tasks, tasks are combined in roles, and roles are assigned to users. Access to a set of modified forms and reports is also controlled via security and assigned at the user level. Users can be granted access to one or more Dynamics GP companies and they can be assigned different roles within each GP company.

At the lowest level, GP grants security to individual operations like accessing a window, generating a report, or posting a transaction. These operations are combined into discreet tasks. For example, the default task ADMIN_FIN_001 has the description "Setup General Ledger" and provides access to security operations like General Ledger Setup, Account Category Setup, Account Class Setup, and more.

GP default tasks are generally broken up into a few segments that correspond to Action Pane items. It's helpful to get a basic understanding of these. The general task breakouts are:

- **ADMIN** – Administrative, setup, and utility tasks, including routines. There are further breakdowns like Admin-Company for company related tasks or Admin-Sales for administrative, setup, and utility tasks in the Sales module.
- **CARD** – In GP, cards represent master records. Access to various cards provides access to master records for customers, vendors, chart of accounts, etc.
- **INQ** – Inquiry items in GP are designed to be read only. Granting access to an inquiry window allows a user to view transaction or master record information. Changes are not permitted in inquiry windows.
- **RPT** – Traditionally, report tasks allow users to run reports in GP. Generally, reports mean information designed to be delivered in a printed format. Like inquiry windows, reports are read only. Often, inquiry windows have corresponding reports allowing users to print information from an inquiry. With new reporting options, new RPT roles are also being used to support connections to GP for other types of reporting such as Power BI.
- **TRX** – Transaction windows allow users access to enter, save, and change transactions in Dynamics GP.
- **DEFAULTUSER** – There is a default user task for GP and there may be other default user tasks for various modules like Fixed Assets and Manufacturing. DEFAULTUSER tasks are designed to provide access to basic interface and navigation windows common to a wide variety of users. Like other tasks, DEFAULTUSER can be modified.

There may be other default tasks in a specific instance of GP, but from a design standpoint, these will be the most prevalent.

The default tasks in GP tend to be narrowly defined to provide access to all the elements required for the defined task. The prebuilt roles are a different story. They were designed for ease of operation, allowing a user to complete all elements of a transaction, instead of being designed with segregation of duties in mind.

For example, the standard role "AP Clerk" in Dynamics GP provides access to maintain vendors, enter payables transactions, print payables checks, and post them. This is a classic SoD no-no. Consequently, using the built-in roles is not recommended. Instead, security design should be used to create new roles. Existing tasks can function as the starting point for new roles. While not perfect, building new roles from existing tasks will address roughly 90% of the security needs of most organizations running GP. Tasks can be used to set security for:

Item	Description
Windows	Windows in the selected product.
Reports	Reports in the selected product.
Modified windows	Windows customized using Modifier.
Modified reports	Primary copies of reports created using Report Writer. Note: The Report Writer name of the report appears in the list. The Report Writer name is the one that appears in the title bar of the Screen Output window when printing a report.

Files	Tables in the selected product.
Alternate Microsoft Dynamics GP reports*	Microsoft Dynamics GP reports that have been incorporated into integrating products that have been installed.
Alternate Microsoft Dynamics GP windows*	Microsoft Dynamics GP windows that have been incorporated into integrating products that have been installed.
Modified alternate Microsoft Dynamics GP reports*	Alternate reports that have been modified using Report Writer.
Modified alternate Microsoft Dynamics GP windows*	Alternate windows that have been modified using Modifier.
Custom reports	Secondary copies and new reports created in Report Writer.
Advanced financial reports	Modified advanced financial reports
Series posting permissions	Specific posting tasks for each Microsoft Dynamics GP product purchased.
Customization Tools	Tools used to customize the accounting system, such as Report Writer or the Modifier. New users don't have access to these by default. They need to be granted access.
Microsoft Dynamics GP import **	The Microsoft Dynamics GP Integration Manager. This also sets up security for the Import Utility

	with Microsoft Dynamics GP. New users don't have access to these by default. They need to be granted access.
Document access	Quotes, orders, invoices, returns, and back orders for Sales Order Processing. Standard and drop-ship purchase orders for Purchase Order Processing.
Letters	Letters to customers, employees, and vendors that are available using the Letter Writing Assistant.
Navigation Lists	Default primary lists. Note: If access is restricted to a primary list, access to any list view that is based on that primary list is also restricted.
*These items appear only if using an integrating product and have selected it in the Product list. **These types appear only if the corresponding item is installed and registered.	

Often companies are tempted to start from scratch with new tasks. Unfortunately, GP has some oddly named security operations, including untitled windows, that can make it difficult to identify all the operations required for a task. This makes rebuilding tasks from scratch time consuming and frustrating for both the person doing the rebuilding and the end users. Building new roles from existing tasks and then making small adjustments offers the best blend of security and efficiency.

Fastpath provides a free, Excel-based security matrix built to assist with designing roles in Dynamics GP. It's available to download from: **http://www.gofastpath.com/gp-security-matrix.**

	A	U	V	W	X	Y	Z
1	**Payables and Purchasing**						
2				**Purchasing Inquiry**			
3		CARD_0303 *	CARD_0304*	INQ_PURCH_001*	INQ_PURCH_00 2*	INQ_PURCH_00 3*	INQ_PURCH_00 4*
4	**Role**	Maintain buyers	Maintain customer/vendor relationships	View vendors	View Payables Management transactions	View vendor financial information	View purchase order transactions
5	**Accounting Dept**						
6	AP Manager			X	X	X	X
7	AP Staff			X	X	X	X
8	AR Manager				X		
9	AR Staff			X	X		
10	Controller						

GP's roles and tasks can be copied, renamed and adjusted. We recommend retaining the default roles and tasks for at least a short time to assist with security troubleshooting. It's easy to misunderstand the nature of a security operation and incorrectly remove access.

The ability to post is a security operation separate from any posting window or window with a posting button. For example, users can be granted access to a batch window to review transactions. This window includes a posting button. Selecting the posting button will display an error if underlying posting permission has not been granted.

If a user is assigned multiple roles, all those roles are active at once, potentially creating segregation of duties issues.

Fastpath Assure provides segregation of
duties analysis for Dynamics GP, including
cross role analysis and the ability to
analyze the effects of granting a user
access to multiple roles.

The importance of designing good roles really can't be overstated. A good set of roles provides a solid security foundation and easy adjustments as companies grow and change.

Alternate/Modified Forms and Reports

In Dynamics GP, the built-in Forms and Reports cannot be modified. However, they can be copied and changed. Also, add-in applications can provide their own form or report as a replacement for GP's default. Collectively, these are referred to as alternate/modified forms and reports.

Typically, there is a default set of forms and reports assigned to users. If certain users need access to different reports or forms, a new set of alternate/modified forms and reports can be created and assigned to that group of users.

For example, a form might be modified to add a field and a report customized to include that field. If all users will only use the new form and report, access can be granted in the default set of forms and reports. If some users need the new form, but other users need the old form, then two sets of permissions are needed for forms and reports. Users can be granted access to one set or the other, giving them access to the new form and report or the old. They can't belong to both.

Managing more than a couple of alternate/modified forms and reports dictionaries becomes cumbersome and difficult to troubleshoot. Minimize the number of alternate/modified report sets for easier management.

User Classes

User Classes are a holdover from a previous security model with only limited security application in Dynamics GP. A user can be assigned to a single class. Classes may be used as part of Field Level Security or Account Security, but they are not a primary security feature.

Field Level Security

In Dynamics GP, access is granted to an entire security operation like a form or report. Field Level Security can provide a deeper level of security by restricting access to specific fields, buttons, or other elements on a form. For example, since commission is often calculated using the Salesperson field on a sales order transaction, companies may want to restrict changes to this field, while still allowing other changes to a transaction.

Field level security is assigned to a user or class, not to a role. Essentially, it represents additional restrictions on specific users or classes in specific forms. Field level security is built by selecting individual elements to restrict and applying rules to those elements. Those rules can include:

- Requiring a password before a user can enter a field
- Requiring a password after a user exits a field

- Warning before entering a field
- Locking a field to prevent changes
- Disabling a field to prevent editing
- Requiring a password before a window is displayed
- Disabling access to a window with the system administrator password
- Requiring a password before any of the windows on a form can be accessed
- Disabling a window and any included forms

 Field level security passwords are not user specific, but are tied to the element being protected. One password is used to protect an element for all users.

The nature of field level security is that access must be specifically denied to individual elements and those settings will vary wildly from company to company. Additionally, getting this access set correctly can be tricky. Consequently, field level security is generally viewed as a compensating control for select areas where application security is insufficient. Auditors generally want to test that field level security settings operate as designed.

Account Security

Account Security provides a way to restrict user access to a defined set of accounts in the chart of accounts. For example, this is often used when companies want to restrict users to accounts related to their own department. In our experience, is this not a widely-used feature. The setup and maintenance tend to be cumbersome and turning this on without proper setup can deny rights to all accounts in the chart to all users.

With account security, an administrator defines an organizational chart and then assigns users individually or by class. Next, accounts are assigned to users or classes in the hierarchy. Finally, account security is activated in the company setup window.

Account Security is default deny-based security. If a user is not given explicit permission to an account, they don't see that account in the chart. This can make the setup tricky. A request like "a user can only enter AP transactions for their department" sounds easy, especially if the department has its own segment in the chart of accounts. But the offsetting AP account is shared among many departments; access to that account must be explicitly granted or the user won't be able to complete the transaction.

Effectively setting Account Security can be time consuming and frustrating for users as they work through implementation issues. Ultimately, Account Security is either on or off. It can't be turned on for just a subset of users.

If account security is activated on the Company Setup window (**Administration**>**Setup**>**Company**>**Company**) without setting up an organizational hierarchy or adding accounts, it will appear as if the chart of accounts has been deleted for all users except 'sa'. Unchecking **Account Security** will restore access to the chart.

System Password

As part of the installation of Dynamics GP, administrators are asked to set a system password. Setting a system password is optional, but is commonly used. In the context of Dynamics GP, the system password controls access to system-wide setup information, such as setting up new user records, assigning user security, or printing reports that contain that information.

The system password is used to grant access to items in the System Inquiry, System Reports, System Setup and System Utilities menus. This password is system-specific, not user specific; that is, the same password is used by everyone to access items in these menus.

The system password functions as a secondary control, effectively a roadblock. For example, when managing roles, a user would first need permission to access the Security Roles window. When activating the window, the user would be asked to supply the system password before the window will open. Since this is one password for all users accessing a resource, it's not a primary control; it's a secondary control designed as a roadblock for someone who might have improper role access.

 The system password is obscured, not technically encrypted, in the underlying SQL database. There are multiple options to both change and recover the system password, including several publicly available techniques. Consequently, the system password should not be relied on as a primary control.

Functional Passwords

Various Dynamics GP functions also include the ability to set a password to perform a specific task. For example, functional passwords are available to allow a transaction to exceed a customer's credit limit or remove a customer hold. The user has underlying rights to these tasks, but can't perform the task without the task specific password.

 Unlike the system password where the value is at least concealed, task passwords are stored as plain text in SQL server. Direct access to SQL tables should be restricted to prevent users from obtaining these passwords. Also, task passwords tend to be shared when needed for temporary access and should be changed regularly.

Task passwords are also available in the Posting Setup window to require batch approval for specific transactions types.

 If activating batch approval for general ledger transactions, approval is required for ALL GL transactions including those flowing from subledgers.

Workflow

In Dynamics GP, the Workflow feature, commonly called Workflow 2.0 as it replaced a previous, SharePoint based version, is used to control record creation, batch approval, and transaction approval. For example, vendor creation can require approval before finalizing the vendor record, or purchase requisition approval can be routed to different approvers based on criteria like total cost, or who creates the requisition.

The workflow feature uses Active Directory based security instead of GP security. This allows easy approval of workflow actions via email, without the user needing to remember another password, and without the security concerns of a shared task password. Consequently, users who only interact with workflows via email do not need to have a GP user license. Workflow actions can also be approved from inside Dynamics GP, as well as via email. Limited users can approve workflows via navigation lists, while full users can approve via navigation lists or buttons available on transaction and batch windows.

In GP, workflow is a secondary control. Like field level security, the actual workflows are designed differently for each organization. Users submitting items via workflow must have security rights to the underlying action, such as creating a requisition or setting up a vendor, but those rights will be constrained by the workflow rules. Auditors will want to review and test workflows to ensure that they operate as intended.

Many of the items previously addressed by task security and other segregated approval features are being replaced by workflow. These include GL & AP batch approval, credit limit override approval, and purchase order approval. Workflow has clearly emerged as the first choice for addressing supplemental security requirements in Dynamics GP.

Other Security

Microsoft Dynamics GP also includes other security areas separate from primary role and task based security. These include separate security for managing OData connections and pre-workflow security measures that may still be appropriate for some organizations. Additionally, there are other products that can improve the operation and management of security in Dynamics GP.

Pre-Workflow Security Features

There are some additional security features in GP that are less comprehensive than workflow, but offer features that overlap workflow. These items were introduced prior to Workflow 2.0 and are generally deprecated by organizations in favor of workflow. These include:

- **Purchase Order Enhancements** – Optional Purchase order approval module with approvals available only inside of GP and integration with the Encumbrances module.
- **Sales Fulfillment Process Holds** – User-defined restrictions that control the processing of sales documents at different stages of the sales cycle including options like management approval and passwords to release holds.

OData

OData is a standardized protocol for creating and consuming data APIs. OData builds on core protocols like HTTP and commonly accepted methodologies like REST. The result is a uniform way to expose full-featured data APIs.

For the accountants in the room, this means that an OData service has been built to allow secure access to Dynamics GP. Once the service is deployed it can be used to securely select data (SQL tables, SQL Views, and SQL stored procs) for use in Power BI, Microsoft Excel, Tableau, or other applications that can access information via OData.

OData security in Dynamics GP is both separate and intertwined with GP security. OData security is effectively setup in 3 layers, and access is denied by default. Once the OData service has been deployed, an administrator must first select what information will be made available via OData. The selection is made by marking GP's underlying SQL tables, views, and/or store procedures available for OData. Next, those items are published in GP. Publishing provides a URL used to access the required information. Finally, users must be granted appropriate access via roles and associated tasks in GP.

Unlike workflow, OData security is a hybrid of GP security and Active Directory based access. OData access is available to GP users, but that access is provided via Active Directory. GP users need to have an Active Directory user name assigned in user setup to connect an Active Directory login with a GP user. GP includes roles and tasks for accessing OData, and new roles and tasks can be built to support additional OData access.

OData is new and has some limitations; still it represents a significant step in making GP data securely available outside the application.

Single Sign On
Single sign on is a key security control helpful in preventing orphaned users and being able to provide a unified view of application access.

37

The virtues of single sign on are praised in the Dynamics GP *Planning for Security* manual[4], but Dynamics GP does not provide single sign on options except for web client users. Even then, the process is a bit disjointed.

The only answer for complete single sign on for Dynamics GP is Config AD from Fastpath. Config AD provides single sign on for GP users with their Active Directory login. After clicking the Dynamics GP icon, users are authenticated via AD and brought directly into Dynamics GP. Optionally, users can be asked to re-enter their Active Directory login again for extra security. Config AD provides additional controls including temporary access to roles. Roles can be configured to expire for users in Config AD. This is perfect for temporary access for events like vacations, leave, or emergencies. More information is available at **http://www.gofastpath.com**.

Deny Based Security

GP doesn't provide many options to override role based security. A few features exist, like field level security, but it can be extremely granular. In many scenarios, companies want similar roles with small differences between those roles. For example, a payables entry role may be the same as a payables supervisor role with a difference of only a few permissions. One option for dealing with this scenario is to copy a role and make changes to the copy.

Another option is Deny Based Security, a feature of GP Power Tools. GP Power Tools is managed by Winthrop Dexterity Consulting and distributed by Mekorma. It provides a suite of tools for enhancing

---

[4] *Planning for Security*, page 17, https://www.microsoft.com/en-us/download/details.aspx?id=34666

many items in GP. Deny Based Security is one of those enhancements.

Deny based security is assigned at the user level and provides the option to explicitly deny access to a security operation, overriding role access. Note that this only works one way, it provides additional security restrictions, it doesn't provide additional security access.

To illustrate how this works, consider our scenario from earlier in this section. Instead of maintaining two roles, one for a payables entry user and one for a payables supervisor, a single role could be created for the supervisor, access provided to both users, and deny based security used to further restrict the payables user's access.

Deny based security is even designed to continue working if the product is uninstalled. More information can be found on deny based security at: **http://www.winthropdc.com/products_GPPT.htm**.

'sa', 'Dynsa', and the Power User Role

In SQL Server, the primary administrator account is 'sa', short for System Administrator. This is a special account in SQL Server with default access to all databases, including non-GP databases, and the ability to perform any operation in SQL server. While 'sa' can be restricted, there are still some third-party options that require the use of 'sa', at least for installation. There are also some installation tasks that are just easier with 'sa' because using 'sa' effectively eliminates security as an issue, making installation more likely to succeed and easier to troubleshoot should it fail.

The use of 'sa' should be severely restricted in organizations. The only real need for 'sa' is during initial installation and subsequent upgrades. Access to 'sa' is not required to add users, manage security, or make backups. Any user with a full license can be granted permission to perform these operations. Details are covered in Chapter 3 of this book, but for design purposes, the 'sa' user should be absolutely minimized.

Another required user is DYNSA, or the Dynamics System Administrator. DYNSA is created by default and was designed as the GP database administrator with access to all GP databases. DYNSA is a holdover from Dynamics GP's pre-SQL Server roots when it was the primary administrator account. Now it's a special account with upgraded access, but frankly, a user account can be configured with the same access while also providing greater visibility to the user making changes. DYNSA should also be severely restricted and used minimally.

Finally, there is a Power User role in Dynamics GP. Officially, it is a role, but this is a misnomer in that roles contain specifically assigned access via tasks, while Power User is more of a security override. For simplicity, we'll continue to call it a role, as Microsoft does, but the differences are important. Instead of checking to see if a user has access, GP sees the Power User role and skips the security check.

 When running security reports in GP, 'sa', 'DYNSA', and Power Users do NOT show on those reports. It is important to include a list of these users when indicating who has access to specific GP operations.

Power User access can be assigned via user security. Both 'sa' and 'DYNSA' are assigned as Power Users by default. Power User provides access to all Dynamics GP. Some items, like adding users, require additional SQL permissions in addition to Dynamics GP permissions, but for GP operations, Power User is king.

We recommend severely restricting the Power User role as well. The use of the Power User role creates significant, pervasive, segregation of duties problems in Dynamics GP. We recommend separating GP administration from master record creation and transactions to make the use of Power User unnecessary.

Fastpath offers a free whitepaper on *Minimizing the Use of 'sa' in Microsoft Dynamics GP* at:
http://www.gofastpath.com/blog/fastpath-white-paper-minimizing-the-use-of-sa-in-microsoft-dynamics-gp.

Security Reporting

GP includes several security reports that can be useful as part of security design. Most of these are found in **Administration>Reports>System>Security**. The **User Security** report is one of the most comprehensive. Also, the **Unassigned Security Operations** report will show security operations not assigned to tasks.

One thing that can be very difficult to accomplish with GP reports is identifying segregation of duties issues, even at the role level. GP's security reports don't easily export to Excel and it requires a lot of back and forth to identify any SoD issues within a role. Cross-role

SoD conflicts are even harder. Fastpath Assure analyzes GP security and can show conflicts in a role, across roles, and at the user level regardless of roles. This may be the hardest thing to accomplish in security design without the help of an outside application. More details on Assure are available at **https://www.gofastpath.com**.

{3}

ACCESS CONTROL

- Role Management
- User Provisioning

In this chapter, we'll look at managing application access for users. As we look at access control, we will get into user provisioning, the process of authorizing and adding users. We will also touch on assigning roles, a part of role management.

In the next chapter, we'll dig deeper into controlling what users can do once they have access. Here we are focused on managing user creation, removal, and connections.

Principles

Authorization

A key piece of ERP security is preventing unauthorized users from accessing the accounting application, essentially controlling the perimeter. In the case of on premise or hybrid installations, this includes controlling physical access to the server, managing certificates, configuring firewalls, and controlling network access among other activities. For hosted or cloud applications, server-side security primarily rests with the cloud provider. Managing server security, certificates, and infrastructure is generally the responsibility of the cloud provider.

It's important that the addition of new users and their respective security be authorized. This is a frontline control, so there needs to be a process in place to authorize new users and their security roles. Fortunately, this is a process many companies handle well.

Similarly, there needs to be a process to authorize changes to a user's access as people move into new roles and change departments. Often, the change process in mid-market firms isn't as consistent as the process for new users.

Orphaned Users

Being able to demonstrate that user additions and changes were properly approved goes hand in hand with ensuring that terminated users are removed in a timely manner. Users should be terminated in the ERP system at the time the individual leaves the organization or when a change in status would require terminating their access. Orphaned users, that is, terminated users with active logins, represent a significant security risk. Terminated users may be inactivated or deleted in Dynamics GP. Deleting a user in GP does not remove the user's ID from any transactions tied to that user.

There are valid arguments for disabling versus deleting users and we recommend that firms should work with their auditors to identify a preferred method. Deleting users is often preferred because it eliminates any risk of a terminated user being inadvertently reactivated. Conversely, disabling users may be preferred because the user's security settings can be preserved allowing auditors to test security and compare a user's access to that user's transactions.

Missed notification is a major source of orphaned users. It's important that companies have a mechanism to communicate when users leave the organization. Often that mechanism is an email, but email is unreliable. Emails get missed, end up in the junk folder, and don't provide a confirmation that the action was completed. Because of this, a regular, periodic review of active users is required.

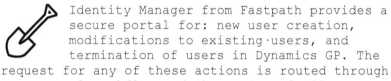 Identity Manager from Fastpath provides a secure portal for: new user creation, modifications to existing·users, and termination of users in Dynamics GP. The request for any of these actions is routed through an approval workflow and then automatically processed in GP to provide an audit trail of requests and approvals.

Reviews

Access reviews are key controls designed to ensure that access controls are operating properly. Managers should be reviewing which users have access and confirming that only appropriate users are represented.

Access reviews should be performed on a regular basis. The schedule may vary from company to company, but access reviews should occur annually at the absolute minimum.

Once a well-managed and designed system of roles and permission management is established, customers may want to move to a model of only auditing role and permission changes on a quarterly basis, and performing a full audit annually.

Additionally, it's important that companies provide evidence that the reviews are being done in a timely manner in the form of physical or electronic sign-off. These access reviews provide the detective control to mitigate the same risk as the preventative provisioning controls discussed above. Controlling access is a primary level of defense. Validating that access control processes are being performed, as evidenced by access reviews, provides another layer of protection.

Access Considerations

External control is important. Managing user access to a firm's ERP system is a key control, but there can be additional controls available to help provide defense in depth. For example, on premise applications may have a VPN as additional defense. The VPN provides an additional layer of access security. The decisions that an organization makes when choosing which options to use to control access should be risk based and tied to the organization's needs.

Related to access controls are settings like password complexity. Strong external controls can be bypassed if weak password security is allowed. Similarly, minimizing users assigned to the Power User role or given access to the 'sa' password is critically important to limiting access to the system.

Fastpath Assure for Dynamics GP provides tools and reports out-of-the-box for access reviews and electronic signatures to provide evidence of those reviews.

Integrating Applications and Services

Another piece of external security is access by integrating applications or services. It's important to understand the security given to third-party applications that plug into the ERP system and ensuring that those applications have the minimum security required. It's not uncommon for integrating applications to be connected using the 'sa' user. This is usually done as a convenience. Using 'sa' typically ensures that security is not an issue for the integrating application, but using 'sa' this way creates huge security holes and can make it extremely difficult to change the 'sa' password later.

Application

Let's look at applying many of these ideas inside of Dynamics GP. In this chapter, we're just looking at the basics of access. In the next chapter, we will get deeper into specifics, like assigning roles. More information about setup options comes later in this chapter, but to get started, let's create a user in Dynamics GP

User Creation

Dynamics GP allows different kinds of users including:

- **Full Users** – Concurrent user license with full read/write access to Dynamics GP and limited only by security settings. This is the most expensive GP license.

- **Limited Users** – Concurrent user license where users can view (read) all information in Dynamics GP, but can only enter information related to their user. Essentially these are concurrent users with all the rights of self-serve users and additional view access. These users' access can be further limited by GP security and there are specific roles included for limited users.

- **Self-Serve Users** – Named user licenses where users can see and enter information for their own user only. This can be further limited by GP security. Self-Serve user licenses are the least expensive licensing option for Dynamics GP. With appropriate permission, self-serve users can enter or access these items for their user:

  o Address
  o Dependents
  o Emergency contacts
  o Title/Position history
  o W-4/Direct Deposit account changes
  o View benefits and employee contributions
  o Distribution changes
  o Skills/Training/Certification history
  o View/Print Pay stubs
  o Enter time

The traditional Dynamics GP client use SQL Server authentication. Single sign on via active directory is not available. There is an option to use active directory users to access GP, but only via the web client. We'll look at the setup for each type.

To setup a user in Dynamics GP:

1. Login as 'sa' or a user with rights to create users in GP. (We cover this later in the chapter.)
2. Select **Administration>Setup>System>User.**
3. Enter a **User ID**. The User ID is limited to 15 characters.
4. Enter the user's name in **User Name**.
5. Optionally enter or select the **Class ID**. User classes are a holdover from a previous security model with only limited security application in Dynamics GP. A user can be assigned to a single class. Classes may be used as part of field level security or account security, but they are not a primary security feature.
6. Set **Status** equal to **Active.**
7. Set **User Type** equal to **Full**. This is where alternative license types can be selected.
8. Optionally select a **Home Page Role** to provide a default set of metrics on the user's home screen.
9. In the SQL Server tab below, enter an initial password for the user in the **Password** field. Passwords in Dynamics GP are limited to 15 characters.
10. Reenter the password in **Confirm Password.**
11. Optionally check the **Enforce Password Policy** to enforce SQL Server password rules.

o Optionally check **Enforce Password Expiration** to force passwords to expire based on SQL Server expiration rules.

If **Enforce Password Expiration** is checked, SQL Server will expire passwords based on rules set in SQL. Unlike Windows, SQL Server expires passwords without warning.

A free, user developed tool to warn users at login that their password will expire soon is available at: http://mbsguru.blogspot.com/2009/12/passwo rd-expiration-prompt-using-vst-to.html. Additionally, there is a SQL query designed to show expiration dates available at: https://community.dynamics.com/gp/b/gpmarianogomez/ archive/2010/07/15/enforcing-password-policy-with- microsoft-dynamics-gp.

o Optionally check **Change Password Next Login** to force this user to change their password from the initial one entered during user setup.

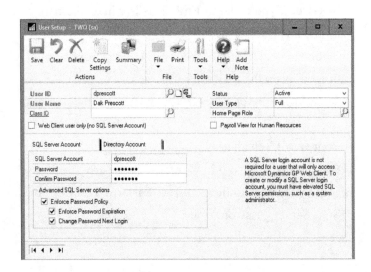

12. If the user will need to connect to GP via the web client, in addition to the traditional client, or if the user will need to connect to other Dynamics GP services like OData or Power BI:
    o Select the **Directory Account** tab.
    o Look up and select the user's corresponding Active Directory account.
13. Click **Save** to save the user.

Adding a Web Client Only User

Regular users can access Dynamics GP via the traditional client or the web client. To set up a web client only user:

1. Login as 'sa' or a user with rights to create users in GP. (We cover this later in the chapter.)
2. Select **Administration>Setup>System>User.**
3. Enter a **User ID**. The User ID is limited to 15 characters.
4. Enter the user's name in **User Name**.
5. Optionally enter or select the **Class ID**. User classes are a holdover from a previous security model with only limited security application in Dynamics GP. A user can be assigned to a single class. Classes may be used as part of field level security or account security, but they are not a primary security feature.
6. Check the box marked **Web Client user only (no SQL Server Account).**
7. Set **Status** equal to **Active.**
8. Set **User Type** equal to **Full**. This is where alternative license types can be selected.

9. Optionally select a **Home Page Role** to provide a default set of metrics on the user's home screen.

10. Select the **Directory Account** tab.

11. Look up and select the user's corresponding Active Directory account

12. Click **Save** to save the user.

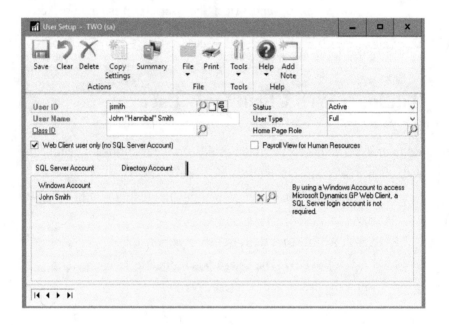

The only answer for complete single sign on for Dynamics GP is Config AD from Fastpath. Config AD provides single sign on for GP users with their Active Directory login. More information is available at **http://www.gofastpath.com/by-erp/microsoft-dynamics/dynamics-gp**.

Granting Company Access

Creating a user allows them to log in but doesn't grant any access. In the next chapter, we'll cover security setup, including assigning roles to users. Before that however, a user needs to be granted access to at least one company in Dynamics GP. Assigning a company is part of the minimum setup required for a user to access Dynamics GP so we've included it here.

To add a user to a company:

1. Login as 'sa' or a user with rights to create users in GP.
2. Select **Administration>Setup>System>User Access.**
3. Select a user from the list on the left. Web client only users are marked with an asterisk.
4. Mark the **Access** box next to one or more companies to grant access.
5. Click **OK**.

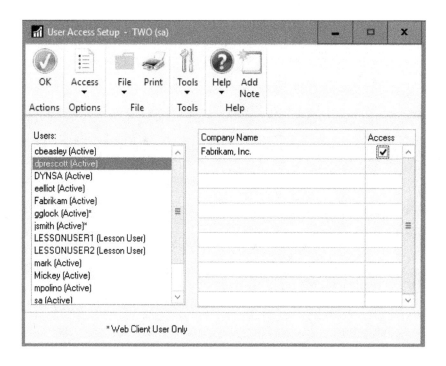

Deleting or Disabling Users

Dynamics GP provides the option to disable or delete a user. The selection of one option or another depends on the company's specific policies. To disable a user in Dynamics GP:

1. Login as 'sa' or a user with rights to create users in GP.
2. Select **Administration>Setup>System>Users.**
3. Enter or look up the appropriate user ID.
4. Change the **Status** from **Active** to **Inactive.**
5. Click **Save.**

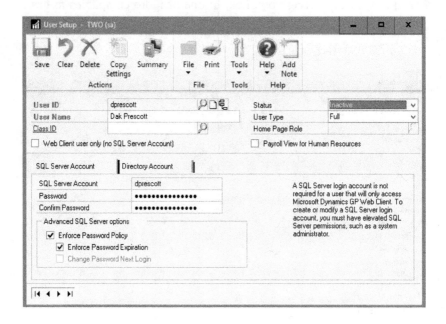

To reactivate a user, simply change status back to **Active**.

To delete a user:

1. Login as 'sa' or a user with rights to create users in GP.
2. Select **Administration>Setup>System>Users.**
3. Enter or look up the appropriate user ID.
4. Select the button marked **Delete** from the menu bar at the top.

The delete button removes the user from Dynamics GP and from SQL Server. It also removes all settings and assignments for the deleted user.

Remembering User and Password

GP includes optional settings to remember a user's ID and the user's password at login. Use of these settings is not recommended. Retaining the password can compromise Dynamics GP security. There are two parts to this feature, a master switch and a user setting. If the master switch is activated, the user can select to remember their user ID and password for future logins by checking the box marked **Remember user and password**.

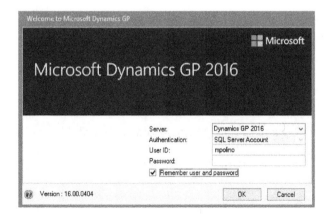

There is no option to only remember the user ID. Disabling this feature is recommended to avoid compromising security in GP. To disable the master switch for remembering the user:

1. Select **Administration>Setup>System>System Preferences**
2. Uncheck the box next to **Enable Remember User.**
3. Click **OK**.

Password Management

Dynamics GP users can manage their own passwords in the application. Navigating to **User Preferences>Passwords** opens a window where a user can enter their old password, new password, and confirm the new password.

GP's password complexity and expiration are driven by SQL Server rules. Since those are often outside of the control of the GP administrator, we won't dwell on that here, but a new password needs to conform to SQL's complexity rules if the related boxes are checked for the user ID.

GP passwords are limited to a maximum length of 15 characters.

Typically, users are able remove their login and reenter GP if they exit without logging out or are otherwise disconnected from the GP client. If a user loses their connection to GP, GP will provide a message on login and options to re-login. To reestablish a login after disconnection:

1. Sign in to Microsoft Dynamics GP.
2. A window will open indicating the user is logged in and offering to let the user view logins.

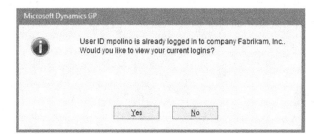

3. Click **Yes** to view existing logins.

4. Select the user and click **Delete** to remove the session.

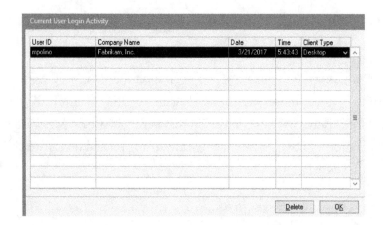

5. The GP login screen will reappear. Click **OK** to log in.

System Administrator – 'sa'

By default, the SQL Server System Administrator user, 'sa', has full control over the SQL instance and full access to Dynamics GP. The 'sa' user is typically used for the installation of Dynamics GP and any related applications. In many organizations, 'sa' is also used for the creation of users, business alerts, and other functions. Many users and even some GP consultants believe that 'sa' is required to setup new users and perform other functions. It is not. The 'sa' user is only required for installation.

```
Technically 'sa' may not be required for
installation, however, there can be issues
with other logins, even if they have the
same rights as 'sa'. As a result, 'sa' is
```

still recommended for installation.

Using 'sa' to create users is not recommended because the 'sa' user is not tied to a specific individual. Anyone with the password can log in as 'sa' making it difficult to tell which user is making changes.

Options for setting up another user with permission to create GP users are detailed in the Dynamics GP *Planning for Security Manual*[5]. One difference is that permission needs to be granted in SQL Server for underlying access and then in GP for specific access.

Dynamics GP *Planning for Security* lists four options for adding new users. Option 1 is to use 'sa'. Since 'sa' doesn't tie back to an individual, this is not an ideal choice. Options 3 and 4 are more complicated, but still closely related to option 2. Because of that, we'll illustrate option 2, namely:

*Assign the specific Microsoft Dynamics GP Administrator(s) SQL Login account to the **SysAdmin** fixed server role. With this option, the Microsoft Dynamics GP administrator can be any user account within the Microsoft Dynamics GP application.*

To set this up:

1. Identify a GP user that will be allowed to create users. This must be a full licensed, SQL-based GP user, not a web-client only user, not a limited user, and not a self-serve user.
2. Login to SQL Server Management Studio (SSMS) with sysadmin rights and connect to the server where GP is

---

[5] Dynamics GP Planning for Security, Page 35

installed. The 'sa' user can be used here, or another user with sysadmin rights. A GP user login cannot be used to login to SQL.

3. In SSMS, navigate to **Security** on the main tree (not security under one of the databases).

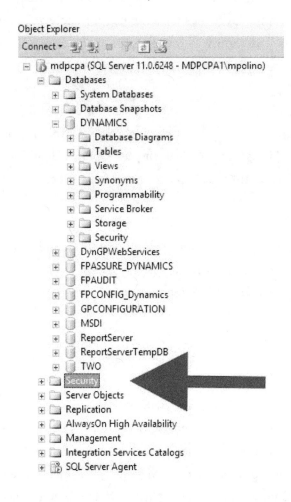

4. Use the + buttons to expand **Security** and **Logins.**

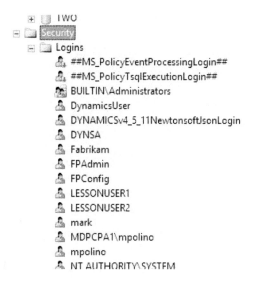

5. Find the user that will be allowed to create GP users. For this example, I'm selecting the user mpolino.

6. **Right-click** on the user that will be allowed to create GP users and select **Properties** to open the **Login Properties Window**.

7. In the **Login Properties** window select **Server Roles.**

8. On the **Server Roles** page, check the box next to **sysadmin** and click **Ok.**

The user now has the appropriate SQL permission to add users in GP. They still need access to the user setup window via roles to be able to add a user in GP.

Database administrators (DBA) are often not fans of assigning a user to the fixed SQL sysadmin role because designating a user as a sysadmin typically gives them total control over a database, but that is not the case with a GP user. The GP user's password is transformed and encrypted prior to sending it to SQL. This means that the password that SQL sees is not the same as the GP password. When a user logs in to GP, their password is unencrypted to allow GP to interact with SQL. Consequently, GP users cannot directly access SQL with their GP login credentials.

A GP user's access to the power of sysadmin is limited to those tasks in GP that require sysadmin rights. The user is constrained in that they can only interact with SQL within the tasks available in GP. A GP user with sysadmin rights is still bound by GP security. A GP user could be given this access to create users, but not given access to assign or change permission. Additionally, a GP user without rights to the user setup window can't assign users simply because they have the sysadmin fixed server role.

Using the 'sa' user is dangerous because it offers total control and a level of anonymity. If multiple users have the 'sa' password, figuring out who used 'sa' to perform a task becomes extremely difficult, if not impossible. Once a DBA becomes comfortable with the fact that setting a few GP users as sysadmins won't give them unfettered access to SQL, this option makes it much easier to limit the use of 'sa'.

Orphaned Users and Licensing

As we've mentioned, eliminating orphaned users is an important control point. This includes reviewing users and their licenses to review for orphaned users and appropriate license distribution. To review users and their licenses:

1. Select **Administration>Setup>System>User.**
2. Click the box marked **Summary** in the menu bar.

GP will provide an inquiry window with a summary of licenses and a list of users, their license level, and companies they have access to.

The same information is available in a printable report at **Administration>Reports>System>User>User Access.**

 Config AD also works to elminate orphaned users. Users deleted or inactivated in active directory are automatically deleted or inactivated, based on Config AD settings, in Dynamics GP. More information is available at: **http://www.gofastpath.com/by-erp/microsoft-dynamics/dynamics-gp.**

User Provisioning

While user creation, modification, and removal are relatively straightforward tasks in Dynamics GP, controlling those tasks, and proving authorization, can be much more difficult. Typically, role and task requests and approvals happen separately from GP, via email or some other mechanism. This makes it difficult to tie requests to actions in GP and ensure that operations are carried out. Workflows are not available in Dynamics GP for user creation.

Identity Manager from Fastpath provides a user provisioning option to address this. With Identity Manager, a user makes a request to create, changes or terminate a user. The request is routed through an approval workflow, and when the approval flow is complete, Identity Manager makes the update automatically in Dynamics GP.

Identity Manager tracks the request, the requester, and the approval chain for later auditing and review against changes in GP. Since requested actions happen automatically once the approval chain is complete, the risk of lost requests and unauthorized changes is significantly reduced.

{4}

SECURITY SETUP

- Role Management
- User Provisioning
- Emergency Access Management

A solid process map and a well thought out security design significantly improve the process of building roles. With the up-front work done, administrators can focus on assigning appropriate permissions to roles and assigning roles to users, instead of trying to make security decisions on the fly during setup. In this chapter, we'll look at permissions, roles, and users in the context of preventative controls.

As we talked about before, assigning roles to users, and understanding the underlying permission, is an important part of both user provisioning and role management. We also dig into emergency access management. That is, the process for managing temporary or unusual permissions.

Principles

Preventative Controls

Application security is the key preventative control in any ERP system. Security assignments with proper segregation of duties are designed to prevent misstatements, fraud, and errors before transactions are completely committed. Additional preventative controls like system user access, approval workflows, and global permissions work in concert with roles and permissions to provide a secure framework.

Roles and Least Privilege

Roles are the primary system control component. They are often the primary preventative control. As we discussed in design, ideally, they should be as free from segregation of duties conflicts as reasonably possible. Roles should also be built following the principle of least privilege, giving users just enough access to do their jobs, but no more. Good role design is usually a trade-off between security and efficiency.

In Chapter 2, we looked at documenting processes and using those processes to design roles. We then discussed mapping those roles to job functions and users. In this chapter, we're looking at moving from role design to role creation and actual assignment to users. A key piece, and one that can be difficult to get right in design, is segregation of duties. Ensuring that sufficient user separation exists in accounting processes is a central focus in reducing fraud, misstatements, and errors.

While it's important to segregate duties as much as possible in design, it can be tough to catch everything during the design phase. Applying multiple roles to a user can create cross-role SoD conflicts that are tough to identify. Part of building and applying roles is to test and review the security setup to identify conflicts that the design may have missed.

Ideally, security should be setup in a test environment to validate the design. Security should be assigned to tasks, task to roles, and roles applied to users in test. For GP, we do NOT recommend using the built-in security roles. They are unlikely to fit any specific company and contain significant segregation of duties issues. Instead, standard roles should be copied to create new roles that can be modified to fit the design and later adjusted as security needs change.

While roles are often assigned to users when they are created, few firms spend the time to get roles right during implementation. Often companies need to revisit security roles later. In our examples, we'll be applying roles to existing users, but this process also works fine for assigning roles to new users.

 Fastpath Assure simplifies the process of understanding security by showing effective security for users and indicating the roles and tasks behind effective permission.

Emergency Access

An often-overlooked area is emergency access. It's not unusual for organizations to need temporary users, like consultants, or to

69

temporarily provide different access when a user is out due to circumstances like vacations or leave.

Requests for temporary access should be approved and have a defined time limit. This is usually where ERP systems have problems and Dynamics GP is no exception. Roles can be assigned to a user on a temporary basis, but there is no mechanism to automatically revoke or expire access. Fastpath's Identity Manager solution provides options for approval and management of temporary access, including access removal on expiration. The use of additional options, like Identity Manager from Fastpath, provides the best path for managing emergency access in Dynamics GP.

Application

Assigning Roles to Users

With good design, it's easier to properly assign roles to users. We'll dig deeper into roles in a minute, but after setting up a user, assigning roles is the next step.

1. Select **Administration >Setup>System>User Security**.
2. Use the lookup button to select a user.
3. Use the dropdown button next to **Company** to select a company.
4. Check one or more boxes next to each role to assign to a user.

Check the **Display Selected Roles** box to only show roles assigned to the user.

5. In the **Alternate/Modified Forms and Reports ID** box, select a set of reports.

6. Click **Save** to save the role assignment.

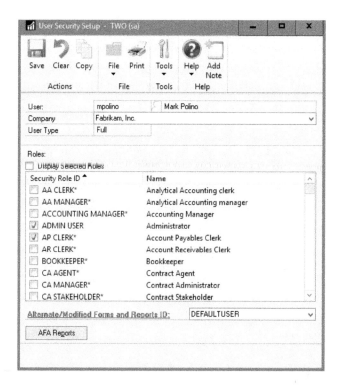

 When the Poweruser role is selected, GP displays the message "Marking the POWERUSER role will give this user access to all application functionality." If the Poweruser role is already selected when adding an additional role, GP provides the notification "This user has access to all application functionality because the POWERUSER role is already marked for this user."

Copying User Access

GP also makes it easy to assign a set of roles by copying security from another user. There are pros and cons to this method. On one hand, copying user access makes setting up a new user faster and easier. It also tends to reduce security access errors, because the setup is the same as a functioning user.

However, copying users can be dangerous. What commonly happens is that a long-time user is given extra permissions over time. This might be in response to an emergency access need or a requirement to fill in for a coworker on leave. As we mentioned in user provisioning, companies do a poor job of removing temporary access, consequently, long-time users often end up with excess access. That excess access is then inadvertently copied down when assigning roles to a user.

It's important to periodically review roles and role assignments to ensure that they still match security design.

To copy user access:

1. Select **Administration>Setup>System>User.**
2. In the **Security Settings** section, use the lookup button to select the user to copy access to.
3. Enter or lookup the user to copy from.
4. Below the Security Settings section are options to copy the **Home Page Role, Home Page Content**, and **Area Pages.**

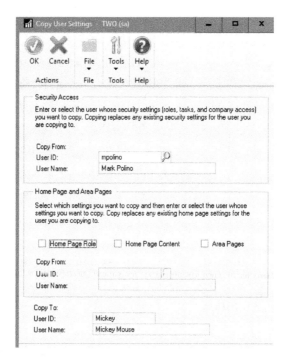

Copy Access to Another Company

The assignment of GP roles to users is done per company. Once roles have been assigned to a user for a given company, those role assignments can be copied to another company for the same user. To copy a user's security to another company:

1. Select **Administration>Setup>System>User Security.**
2. Lookup or enter a user ID.
3. Select a company from the dropdown.
4. Click **Copy** from the menu bar.
5. Check the box next to one or more companies to copy to.
6. Click **Ok.**

Copying a Role

In case the message hasn't gotten through, using the default roles in GP is not recommended. The preferred technique is to create new roles using GP tasks as a base. Good security design is key to making role creation easy. If roles are well designed, role creation is simply an exercise in checking boxes. One option to make role creation easier is to copy and modify an existing role as a way of creating new roles. To copy and modify a role:

1. Select **Administration>Setup>System>Security Roles.**
2. Enter the name for the new role ID. In my example, I used **AP Clerk Modified.**
3. Enter a name for the new role. This is the role that tasks will be copied into.
4. Click the **Copy** button.
5. Lookup and select a role to copy from.

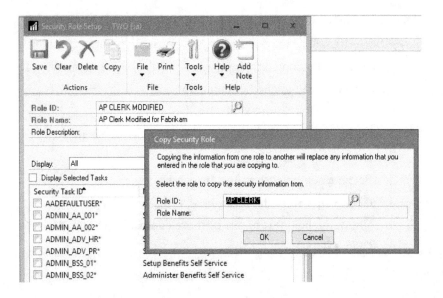

6. Click **OK.**

7. Optionally modify the role description.

8. Modify the new role by removing conflicting tasks and adding new tasks as required.

9. Click **Save** to save the role.

Creating a New Role

It may still be necessary, or preferred in some cases, to create roles from scratch. To create a new role:

1. Select **Administration>Setup>System>Security Roles.**

2. Enter the name for the new role ID.

3. Enter a name for the new role.

4. Optionally enter a role description.

5. Check the box next to each task to be assigned to a role.

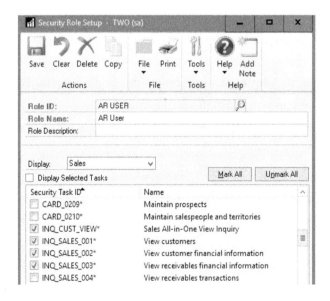

6. Use the **Display** option to filter the tasks shown on the screen to specific modules. This is helpful for reducing the number of tasks to wade through.

7. Check the box for **Display Selected Tasks** to show only tasks added to this role. This is very useful for reviewing assigned tasks.

 Remember to apply the principle of least privilege to role creation. Roles should not contain excess privileges and should have a minimum number of segregation of duties conflicts.

Modifying an Existing Role

We recommend against simply modifying the default roles. It's too easy to break security that way and it's important to balance the need for security against the ability to get work done. Still, once custom roles have been built, it may be necessary to modify them later. To modify a role:

1. Select **Administration>Setup>System>Security Roles.**

2. Lookup and select an existing role.

3. Mark or unmark specific tasks to respectively add or remove tasks to the role.

4. Click **Save** to save the change.

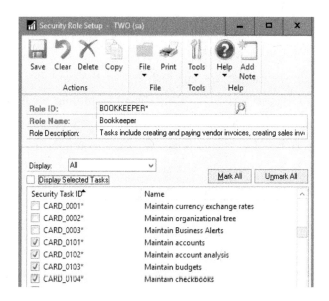

5. Use the **Display** option to filter the tasks shown on the screen to specific modules. This is helpful for reducing the number of tasks to walk through.

6. Check the box for **Display Selected Tasks** to show only tasks added to this role. This is very useful for reviewing assigned tasks.

Creating a task

The prebuilt tasks in Dynamics GP tend to be well designed with enough access to get the task done, but without excessive access. Still, there are times when the prebuilt tasks won't quite suffice and a new task needs to be built from scratch. This is more likely to be the case for security related to an ISV solution.

Like creating a role, creating a task is ultimately a matter of adding security operations to a task. The challenge is there are more options when creating a task. First, there is the selection of a product. Typically, this is Microsoft Dynamics GP, but ISV solutions and Microsoft modules that are not included in the base dictionary are managed individually. This is a significant stumbling block for users that are new to Dynamics GP, especially when trying to find an obscure window to grant access to. For example, Excel Based Budgeting is a GP module with its own dictionary. In the **Product** drop down, Excel Based Budgeting has its own selection option.

The second challenge is type of access being granted. Access can be granted to multiple security elements including:

- **Windows** – access to windows in Dynamics GP, including inquiry windows.
- **Reports** – access to run reports in Dynamics GP

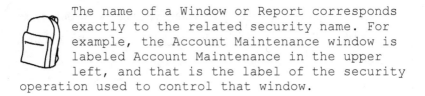 The name of a Window or Report corresponds exactly to the related security name. For example, the Account Maintenance window is labeled Account Maintenance in the upper left, and that is the label of the security operation used to control that window.

- **Files** – access to specific GP tables. Typically, GP users are not restricted at the table level. Information management is usually done at the Window or Report level.
- **Custom Reports** – access to secondary modified reports or new custom reports. Typically, report changes are modified or alternate reports, and are managed via Alternate/Modified Forms and Reports rather than custom reports.
- **Series Posting Permission** – controls the ability to post. The word 'series' here is used to mean 'module' and is different from the GP concepts of transaction, series, and master

posting. These posting options are controlled with Series Posting Permission.

- **Customization Tools** – access to customization tools like Report Writer and Modifier.
- **Microsoft Dynamics GP Import** – security for Integration Manager and the Import Utility. For Integration Manager users also need access to the windows related to the data being integrated.
- **Document Access** - quotes, orders, invoices, returns, and back orders for Sales Order Processing. Standard and drop-ship purchase orders for Purchase Order Processing.
- **Letters** - letters to customers, employees, and vendors that are available using the Letter Writing Assistant.
- **Navigation Lists** - default primary lists. Note: If access is restricted to a primary list, access to any list view that is based on that primary list is also restricted.
- **Service Enabled Procedures** – service based architecture security.

The GP team has provided additional information on security for Service Enabled Procedures at: https://community.dynamics.com/gp/b/dynamics gpengineeringteamblog/archive/2015/04/13/service-based-architecture-service-procedure-security.

- **SQL Objects** – Access to SQL stored procedures and views. Access is typically managed via windows or reports instead of SQL objects.

Not all products will have access to all elements. Back to our example, there is no posting element for the processes around Excel Based

Budgeting, so Series Posting Permission does not show in the Excel Based Budgeting drop down.

The third challenge is the Series. Normally, this corresponds to a GP module. For example, Excel Based Budgeting is accessed via the Financial area from the GP interface. When building a security task, many of the windows for Excel Based Budgeting are listed under the Financial series. This means that it may be necessary to search through multiple series when looking for various windows. Often there may be additional setup windows in the System or Company series.

With that background, let's create a task. For our example, we'll add a new Excel Based Budgeting task. To create a new task:

1. Navigate to **Administration>Setup>System>Security Tasks.**
2. Enter a task name. I used **Test XL Based Budgeting**.
3. Select a category for this task to appear in when adding tasks to roles. I chose **Financial**.
4. Enter a **Task Name**.
5. Enter a **Task Description**.
6. Use the drop down to change **Product** to **Excel Based Budgeting**.
7. Use the drop down to set the **Type** to **Windows**.
8. Use the drop down to set the **Series** to **Financial**.
9. Use the drop down to set the **User Type** to **Full**.

If Limited or Self Service is selected, only
those security permissions available to
Limited or Self Service users respectively,
will appear in the Operations window below.

10. Check the box next to the appropriate permissions. For our example, I've selected all the boxes.

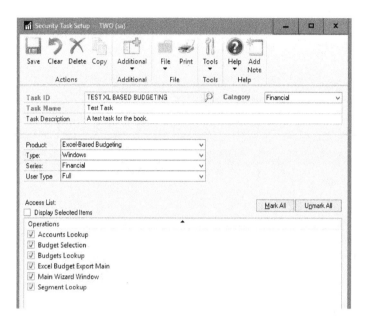

11. Click **Save** to save the task.

12. Use the **Product, Type, Series,** and **User Type** to filter the tasks shown on the screen to specific modules. This is helpful for reducing the number of tasks to wade through.

13. Check the box for **Display Selected Tasks** to show only tasks added to this role. This is very useful for reviewing assigned tasks.

Copying a Task

Like roles, tasks can be created by copying an existing task as a base and then modifying the task. This can be a significant timesaver versus creating a task from scratch. To copy a task:

1. Navigate to **Administration>Setup>System>Security Tasks.**
2. Enter a task name.
3. Click **Copy** on the menu bar.
4. Enter or lookup the Task ID to copy from.

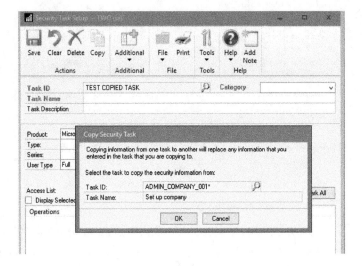

5. Click **OK**.
6. Modify the task as required.
7. Click **Save** to save the task.
8. Use the **Display** option to filter the tasks shown on the screen to specific modules. This is helpful for reducing the number of tasks to walk through.

9. Check the box for **Display Selected Tasks** to show only tasks added to this role. This is very useful for reviewing assigned tasks.

Since it can be difficult to understand the full breath of a task's contents from the security tasks window, the **Print** option on this window will print the security objects assigned to a task.

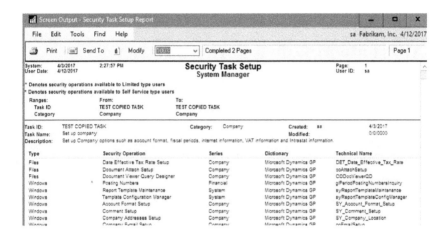

Modifying a Task

Modifying a task works a lot like creating or copying a task. It is not recommended to modify the default tasks. Modifying a default task can break security for users and it can be difficult to return to working security, especially if multiple changes are made. Instead, make a copy, modify the copy, and assign the modified task to a role. To modify a security task:

1. Navigate to **Administration>Setup>System>Security Tasks.**
2. Lookup and select a **Task ID.**

3. Modify the task as required.

4. Click **Save** to save the task.

5. Use the **Product, Type, Series,** and **User Type** to filter the tasks shown on the screen to specific modules. This is helpful for reducing the number of tasks to wade through.

6. Check the box for **Display Selected Tasks** to show only tasks added to this role. This is very useful for reviewing assigned tasks.

Alternate/Modified Forms and Reports

Alternate forms and reports are forms and reports that have been incorporated into integrating products that have been installed. Modified forms and reports are existing Microsoft Dynamics GP forms and reports that have been modified using Report Writer or Modifier.

Alternate/modified forms and reports IDs grant access to groups of alternate/modified forms and reports within Microsoft Dynamics GP. Only one alternate/modified forms and reports ID can be assigned to a user at a time. For the default forms and reports, there are four possible versions of a form/report, but a user can only have access to one of these. Multiple alternate/modified forms and reports IDs allow the assignment of different reports to different users. The four different types are:

Type	Description
Form/Report	The base form or report included with GP
Modified	A modified version of the base form/report
Alternate	A substitute form/report from a 3rd party add in
Alternate Modified	A modified version of the Alternate form/report

Assigning an ID to a user is very easy. It's done as part of setting user security. To set the alternate/modified forms and reports ID:

1. Navigate to **Administration>Setup>System>User Security.**
2. Look up and select a user.
3. Select a company from the drop down.
4. Lookup and select an **Alternate/Modified Forms and Reports ID** below role selection.
5. Click **Save**.

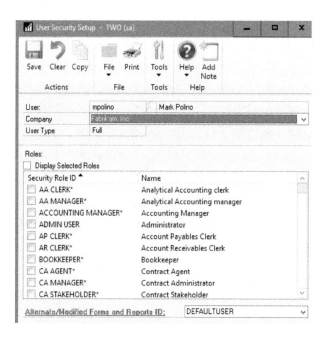

Often, there is only a small number of choices, and in many cases, there may only a be single Alternate/Modified Forms and Reports ID for an entity.

Alternate/Modified Forms and Reports IDs are almost never built from scratch. There are too many choices. Typically, they are modified or copied into a new ID first and then modified.

To manage alternate/modified forms and reports in GP:

1. Select **Administration>Setup>System>Alternate/Modified Forms and Reports.**

     The copy button copies an ID for alternate/modified forms and reports using steps just like copying a role or task.

2. Select a **Type**. Pick **Windows** for GP forms/windows. Select **Reports** for reports. In our example, I know that I have a modified Account History report so I've selected Reports.
3. **Product** and **Series** can be used to limit the selection.
4. Click the plus (+) button next to a module to expand the element. In my example, this is **Financial. Account History** is the only option under **Financial** because it is the only report with modified or alternate options.
5. Select **Microsoft Dynamics GP** or **Microsoft Dynamics GP (modified)** as the report this ID will grant access to.

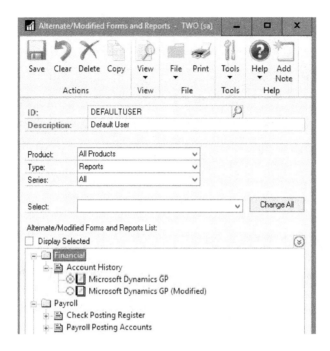

6. Click **Save** to save the report.

An example of an alternate form would be the Project Accounting version of purchase order entry. Users with access to the alternate form have cost category and project fields added to the purchase order entry window.

When viewing GP windows there are typically at least two options for every window, Microsoft Dynamics GP and SmartList. The Microsoft Dynamics GP option is an older, classic window that is generally less useful, and frankly, uglier. SmartList is the newer interface option and provides enhanced sorting, lookup, and filtering options. SmartList is the default and should normally be the right choice if the window is not otherwise modified.

Posting Control

A handful of scenarios present issues for users when setting up security. One of those is posting control. There are a couple of ways to secure posting including batch approval, workflow, field level security, and finally, tasks. We cover batch approval, workflow, and field level security later in this book, but posting control is by far the simplest.

For example, a company wants users to be able to create, but not post, journal entries. Restricting access to the appropriate Series Posting type prevents users from posting. That's it. The other options come with pros and cons that can require difficult process choices. Controlling series posting is by far the simplest option.

SmartList Security

SmartList security is another area that is often difficult for people to secure. SmartLists are ad hoc reports on data contained in Dynamics GP. What's confusing is that SmartList is a product in task setup. It's not included in the base Dynamics GP dictionary. When SmartList is selected as a product, the SmartList Object is available as both a type and a series. With those selections, specific SmartLists display in the access list. Once that is understood, it is much easier to figure out how to adjust security for SmartLists.

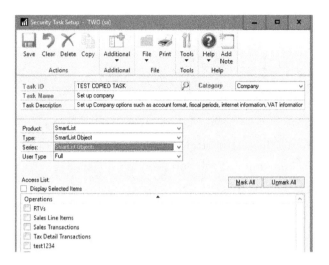

Excel Report Security

Dynamics GP includes a set of refreshable Excel reports. These reports pull data directly from Dynamics GP and use Microsoft Excel to deliver information. Because the reports can be refreshed from Excel, the security mechanism used to access data via Excel is important.

Refreshable Excel report security is different from other GP security settings. Because GP encrypts the login password, GP logins are not available for Excel reports. Excel report security is based on Active Directory logins and are managed via fixed SQL Server roles. GP includes a set of fixed SQL server roles that begin with **RPT** and are designed for refreshable Excel reports. The *System Setup Guide* is available at:

https://technet.microsoft.com/en-us/library/hh686214(v=gp.20).aspx.

The guide contains additional information on setting up and using Excel reports. There are options for assigning reports to individual users or via the use of active directory groups. We won't go into this in depth, but we will do a simple example. To add Excel report permissions:

1) Open SQL Server Management Studio and connect to the server where GP is installed.
2) Drill down to the **GP company database>Security>Users**.
3) Select an **Active Directory** user.
4) Right-Click and select **Properties**.
5) Under **Select a Page** on the left, pick **Membership**.
6) Check the box next to the corresponding rpt role. In this example, I selected **rpt_accounting_manager**.

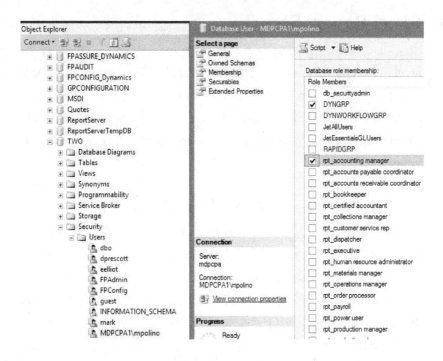

7) Click **OK** to apply security.

OData Security

OData is a resource-based web protocol for querying data. It makes accessing GP data remotely for analysis in products like Tableau or Power BI easier than ever before.

Even better, OData seems to have been built with security in mind. First, the OData connection must be created and secured with an SSL certificate as part of the setup, so there's a solid security base at the core. Second, data must be both selected and published to be available. For example, if a user selects to make payroll data available, but it isn't published, no one can access that data, even with appropriate permission.

Finally, even after data is published, the user must have appropriate role access to a specific set of data to make it available to something like Power BI. In this first release, OData information roughly correlates to the same data sets that were already available in SmartLists and refreshable Excel Reports. It's that same information, now accessible outside the firewall. The OData process is both easier and more secure than trying to lock down externally facing Excel data, while still allowing data access.

To help make all of this happen, GP 2016 comes with a new set of roles and tasks. These are designed to provided user level access to specific information. Security is managed via Active Directory users, not GP users. That is a little different from what most GP security administrators are accustomed to.

We'll take a quick look at setting up OData security. If OData has been properly installed, there is an SSL certificate in place for secure web authentication. Next, we'll select data. To select data for publishing:

1) Select **Administration>System>Setup>OData>Data Sources**.
2) Set the company and object type.
3) Check the box next to objects that will be published.
4) Click **OK.**

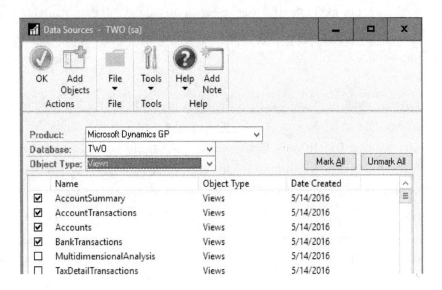

Due to performance issues, do not select too many objects to publish in this release.

Now that these items are available to publish, they need to be published.

To publish an OData element:

1) Select **Administration>System>Setup>OData>Publish OData.**

2) Check **Publish** next to each source to make the data source available. The associated URL to access this data is shown on the right.

3) Click **OK**.

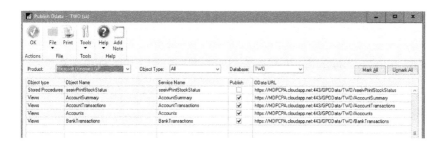

We've selected OData to publish and we've published the data, but it's only available to users with appropriate roles. To apply a built-in role for OData:

1) Select **Administration>System>Setup>User Security**.

2) Enter or lookup a user.

3) Select a company.

4) Scroll down to roles beginning with **OD.**

5) Select the appropriate OData role.

6) Click **Save** when done.

Ultimately, OData access is similar in concept to Excel report access in that predefined roles provide access to data sets and those roles are assigned to users.

Microsoft provides full documentation for OData at: *https://mbs.microsoft.com/Files/customer/ GP/Downloads/ProductReleases/GP2016%20Fea tures.zip.* This documentation includes all the roles and tasks included for OData along with the SQL Views related to each task.

With OData, companies aren't restricted to existing data sources, roles, and tasks. It is possible to create a custom data source for OData and then assign access to a custom task making role assignment easy. To create a custom data source:

1. Select **Administration>System>Setup>OData>Data Sources**.
2. Select **Add Objects** from the menu bar.
3. Select a database and object type.
4. Check the box next to the object(s) to add.

5. Click **Ok** twice.

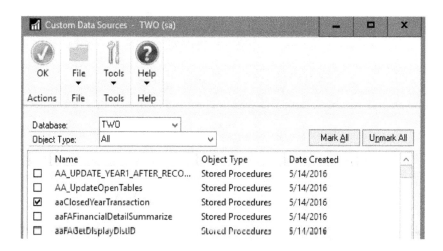

The new custom data source is now available to be added to a task. To add this to a task:

1. Select **Administration>System>Setup>Security Task**.
2. Select or create a task.
3. Select the appropriate product.
4. Set **Type** to SQL Objects.
5. Set **Series** to **Stored Procedures** or **Views** as appropriate.
6. Check the box next to the item that was added.

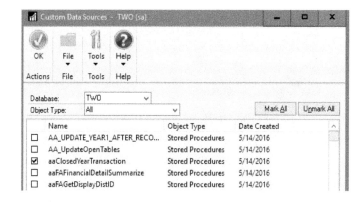

7. Click **OK**.

Now this task can be added to a role just like any other task.

Deleting Security Records

GP offers an option to mass remove roles, tasks, and alternate/modified IDs. This is particularly useful for mass cleanup efforts like removing converted roles from GP after building and assigning new roles.

To mass remove security records:

1. Navigate to **Administration>Utilities>Remove Security Setup Records.**
2. Select the type of records to remove, security roles, security tasks, or alternate/modified forms and reports.
3. Select the range of records to remove.
4. Click **Process**.

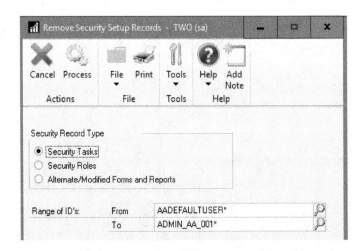

Emergency Access

Another important consideration is emergency access. This usually comes in one of two forms, temporary users and temporary permissions. Temporary users need access for a specified timeframe. This often includes consultants or temporary employees who wouldn't otherwise have access to Dynamics GP. GP doesn't have a good mechanism to address temporary users, so we'll look at a third-party option. Temporary permissions represent elevated or additional permission in GP for a defined period. Usually this is needed when a user is temporarily performing new or additional functions due to vacations, leave, or interim assignments.

With GP's lack of real options around emergency access, Fastpath's Identity Manager tool becomes an important part of the security process. We saw earlier that Identity Manager can securely manage employee creation, changes, and removals via a workflow approval process. As part of that functionality, users can use Identity Manager to set date/time restrictions for GP users when temporary users are required.

All of Identity Manager's changes flow through an approval workflow. Once approved, temporary user or access security is applied in GP. User access is only available during the date and timeframe set. Identity manager automatically removes or disables the user once the expiration date and time pass.

Identity Manager can be used to set date/time restrictions on roles and automatically remove that permission at expiration. This is a great choice for vacation, leave, or other temporary access.

Testing

Testing security changes in a test environment is a leading practice, and this applies to GP as well. Security should be tested in a test environment prior to using new roles and tasks in production.

Part of the challenge with testing is determining what rights users have. GP offers an option to show users, related roles, and task assignments in **Administration>Reports>System>Security>User Security.** But this only explains the roles and tasks assigned to a user, it doesn't drill down to the security operation.

Determining what a user can do is important for reviewing segregation of duties. This can be difficult to do in GP. A lot can be done with reports and custom SmartLists built with SmartList Designer, but it's still a lot of comparing users, roles, tasks, and operations with a segregation of duties ruleset that would need to exist separately from GP. There is another option. Fastpath's Assure tool includes a prebuilt, customizable ruleset designed for GP to show segregation of duties conflicts within roles and across roles. This makes it easy to find and fix SoD issues in the test environment before pushing security to production, and it makes it easy to monitor production over time to ensure that new conflicts aren't being created.

Once security is setup in a test environment and validated, it can be a challenge to move that data to production. If a test company is used in the production environment, it is possible to copy user security from a test company to the production company on a per user basis. This can work well for smaller companies since they are less likely to have a separate test environment and have fewer users in general.

To copy security from a test company to production for a user:

1. Select **Administration>Setup>System>User Security.**
2. Lookup or enter a user ID.
3. Select the test from the dropdown.
4. Click **Copy** from the menu bar.
5. Check the box next to one or more production companies to copy to.
6. Click **Ok**.

Copying security from a test environment to a production environment is more difficult. There isn't a way to do this via the interface. To move data from a test server to a production server involves replacing the contents of the security tables in production with the new setup from the test environment. The tables to be replaced are:

Table Name	Physical Name	Description
sySecurityMSTRRole	SY09100	Master table for Security Roles
sySecurityAssignTaskRole	SY10600	Assignment table for Security Roles to Tasks
sySecurityMSTRTask	SY09000	Master table for Security Tasks
sySecurityAssignTaskOperations	SY10700	Assignment table for Security Tasks to Operations
sySecurityMSTRModAlt	SY09200	Master table for Alternate/Modified Groups
sySecurityAssignModAltOperations	SY10800	Assignment table for Alternate/Modified Operations
sySecurityAssignUserRole	SY10500	Assignment table for Users to Security Roles
sySecurityAssignUserModAlt	SY10550	Assignment table for Users to Alternate/Modified Groups

Optionally, the two tables with Assign User in the name can be skipped and users can be manually assigned to new roles and alternate/modified groups.

Security Reporting

GP offers a set of security reports to help with understanding and documenting security. These reports are found via **Administration>Reports>System>Security** and include:

- **Security Task Setup** – Security operations assigned to each task.
- **Security Role Setup** – Security tasks assigned to each role.
- **Security Role Assignment** – Users assigned to each security role.
- **Security Task Assignment** – Users associated with each security task.
- **User Security** – Users, their assigned role and associated task.
- **Unassigned Security Operations** – a list of security operations not assigned to any task.
- **Alternate/Modified Forms and Reports** – report on the alternate/modified status of windows and reports.

{5}

OTHER CONTROLS & MITIGATION

- Role Management
- User Provisioning
- Monitoring

It never seems to be possible to fit appropriate segregation of duties into application security. Perfect preventative controls are both inefficient and rigid. The use of other system controls and detective controls can provide additional layers of flexible security.

In this chapter, we'll dig into some controls and mitigation options beyond basic application security. Mitigation is used to address shortcomings in role management and user provisioning provided through application security. Often, mitigation involves monitoring and reviewing transactions through tools that we'll look at in this chapter.

Principles

Mitigation

Mitigation doesn't correct a conflict, instead it allows the conflict to exist and creates or identifies other controls that compensate for the risk of excess access. When a firm mitigates a SoD conflict, it accepts the risk associated with a conflict and attempts to compensate via the use of other controls. These other controls can be other application controls, IT controls, or manual control operations.

Common mitigation and detective control options include items like approvals and reviews. A key piece of any detective control is evidence that the control is being performed. For example, if a control is that journal entries need to be approved before posting, there needs to be evidence of an approval. Evidence might include a physical signature, an electronic signature, an email, or other proof.

Often, other features in an application can be used to fill in control gaps and mitigate risks. Features like workflow and approvals can be used to break up a process where other SoD options might not be practical. Audit trail features are useful for change reviews as part of a mitigation process. Likewise, reconciliations are important for identifying and fixing errors, and ideally, preventing them in the future. Reporting in many forms, when combined with related reviews, are a core detective control, but auditors only tend to rely on them when there is evidence that reports are truly being reviewed.

A company's SoD matrix and the map connecting processes to application roles are critical to identifying risks that are not addressed by application security. It is also important to remember that not all risks are created equal, and critical operations for one company may be irrelevant to another. Identifying and focusing on critical access items is an important way to simplify reviews and focus them on items important to the organization.

Once an organization is left with processes that include SoD conflicts, the next step is to identify options to adjust processes, apply detective controls, or find other mitigation options.

For example, a common issue in small payables departments is that payables users have the right to create a vendor and enter a vendor invoice. This opens a risk of redirecting payments to a false vendor. It's often hard to segregate vendor creation and vendor invoice entry in smaller organizations. Common mitigation options would include using a workflow for approval of new vendors, or using a review process where another user who is uninvolved in the operation, reviews a report or audit trail of new vendors against invoices and invoice approvals to validate the vendor's authenticity.

In the Application section of this chapter, we'll look at some options to assist with setting up detective controls and mitigating SoD conflicts in Dynamics GP.

Application

Master Security

An important security consideration in Dynamics GP is the master security switch. Dynamics GP contains a master security switch that is accessed via **Tools>Setup>Company>Company**.

The **Security** checkbox on this window is a master security switch. If this box is not checked, security is not active for this company. It's important to ensure it is checked for each company and access to the **Company Setup** window is properly secured.

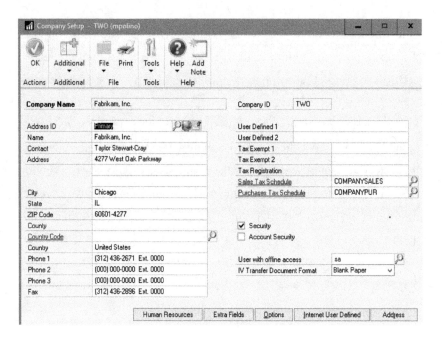

 Do not check the **Account Security** box unless **Account Setup** and **Organizational Security** has been properly setup. If these setups have not been completed and Account Security is checked, access will be denied to the chart of accounts and it will appear that the chart has been deleted. Unchecking the box restores access.

This information is also present on the Company Settings List report found at **Reports>Company>Setup>Company Settings**.

System Password

For certain areas of GP, there is an option to set a System Password. The system password functions as an additional check for users who already have access. The system password is obscured in SQL Server to prevent users from looking it up, but it is not securely encrypted. There are multiple methods available to both change and recover the system password, so it should not be considered a primary security control.

To set the system password:

1. Navigate to **Administration>Setup>System>System Password.**
2. Enter a system password in **New Password**.
3. Repeat the password in **Reenter New Password** and click **OK**.

If a system password is present, certain areas in GP will require it. The areas that are affected by a system password include[6]:

- Security Task Creation/Edits
- Security Roles Creation/Edits
- Alternate/Modified Forms and Reports Creation/Edits
- User Creation/Edits/Deletion
- User Class Creation/Edits
- User Access Management
- User Security (Role Assignment)
- Field Level Security
- System Password Edits
- Activity Tracking
- Currency Definition/Edits/Deletion
- Exchange Management Table
- Multicurrency Access
- Euro Relationships
- Registration Edits
- Business Alerts Creation/Edits/Deletion
- Organization Table Structure Creation/Edits
- Intercompany Setup
- Language Configuration
- Payroll Tax Table Edits/Changes
- Process Server Configuration
- Launch File Edits
- Reporting Tools Setup
- Named Printers Setup/Edits
- Client Update Configuration

---

[6] Richard L. Whaley, *The Dynamics GP Security Handbook*, (Altamonte Springs: Accolade Publications, Inc.), V-4

- SmartList Options Edits
- Activity Tracking Inquiries
- Process Server Status Inquiries
- Reconcile System Tables
- Remove Multicurrency Rates
- Remove Activity Tracking Detail
- Remove Process Server Detail
- Business Alerts Table Maintenance
- User Activity Record Deletion
- Deletion of Companies
- Remove Security Setup Records
- Run System Reports
- Send Users Message

There may be more items depending on specific modules installed. This password is system-specific. Only one password can be created and it is shared among users with access to these menus. The system password can also be changed using this window.

Functional Passwords

Like the system password, GP has other shared passwords used to provide another layer of protection for various functions. For example, a functional password can be required to remove a vendor hold. Like the system password, there is one password per function.

We'll use this as an example. To set a functional password for a vendor hold:

1. Select **Purchasing>Setup>Payables**.

2. In the **Password** section, key a password next to **Remove Vendor Hold**.

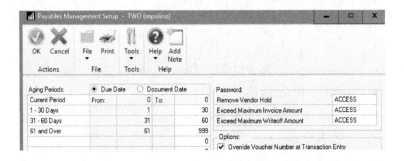

3. Click **OK**.

Functional passwords are often found on setup screens, but not exclusively. They can be easy to miss. For example, the Sales Order Processing Setup window has functional passwords in a grid and it's deeply buried in **Sales>Setup >Sales Order Processing>Options**.

Since a functional password is the same for all users, it is often broadly known in a department. Consequently, these passwords should be changed on a regular basis.

Functional passwords are available throughout the system including[7]:

Receivables

- Exceed Credit Limits
- Remove Customer Hold
- Exceed Maximum Writeoff
- Waive Finance Charge

---

[7] Richard L. Whaley, *The Dynamics GP Security Handbook*, (Altamonte Springs: Accolade Publications, Inc.), V-5 through V-13

Sales Order Processing
- Quotes
  - o Delete Documents
  - o Edit Printed Documents
  - o Override Document Numbers
  - o Void Documents
- Orders
  - o Allow Invoicing of Unfulfilled or Partially Fulfilled Orders
  - o Delete Documents
  - o Edit Printed Documents
  - o Override Document Numbers
  - o Void Documents
- Back Orders
  - o Delete Documents
  - o Edit Printed Documents
  - o Override Document Numbers
  - o Void Documents
- Fulfillment Orders
  - o Delete Documents
  - o Edit Printed Documents
  - o Override Document Numbers
  - o Void Documents
- Returns
  - o Delete Documents
  - o Edit Printed Documents
  - o Override Document Numbers
  - o Override Unit Cost for Returns
  - o Void Documents
- Process Holds

Payables
- Remove Vendor Hold
- Exceed Maximum Invoice Amount
- Exceed Maximum Write-Off Amount

Purchasing
- Allow Receiving Without a Purchase Order
- Change Site ID in Receiving
- Allow Holds/Remove Holds of Purchase Orders
- Allow Editing of Costs in Receiving
- Posting
- Warn when Purchase Order Line Item is not fully invoiced.

Posting Approval

Dynamics GP provides the option to approve batch posting via functional passwords. Posting approval passwords are setup per module. The user who approves the transaction is tracked, but the password is shared, like all functional passwords.

To setup a password for batch posting approval:

1. Select **Administration>Setup>Posting>Posting**.
2. Select a **Series** and **Origin**. For our example, select:
   o Series = Financial
   o Origin = General Entry
3. Check the box next to **Batch Approval**.
4. Enter the password in **Approval Password.**

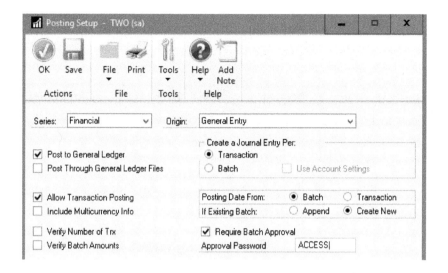

5. Click **OK** to accept the new password.

 There is a significant challenge with this example which is why it was used. If batch approval is activated for General Entry, ALL journal entries, from any modules will NOT post through the GL. They will post TO the GL and stop to wait for GL batch approval, including posting made from subledgers. This often presents a significant barrier to adopting GL approvals this way. Batch approval workflow, discussed later in this chapter, is a better option for journal entry approval.

Account Level Security

Dynamics GP provides another level of security known as Account Level Security or just Account Security. Account security sets restrictions on the accounts available to users. The account security feature can be confusing and it's not unusual for access to be accidently denied to necessary accounts, like shared accounts payable.

Maybe because of issues like this, it's not broadly used. We won't go into great depth, but here is an overview.

Before account security can be applied, **Organizational Structures** need to be created. Organizational Structures define the access that account security uses. For a basic account security setup:

1. Enter up to 4 organizational levels and definitions for each level.

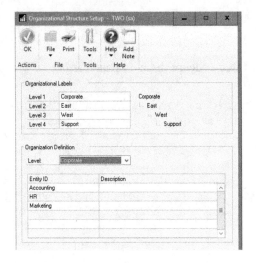

2. Navigate to **Administration>Cards>Organizational Assignments.**
3. Select a label and a level. In my example, I'm selecting **Corporate** and **Accounting**.

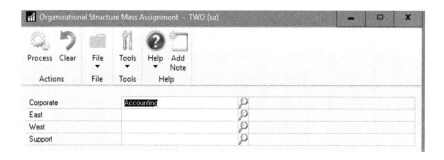

4. Select a company.

5. Mark the box next to **Assign.**

6. Check the box next to **Apply to Parent Levels.**

7. Select a segment ID or account. For this example, pick **Segment ID.**

8. Select a segment.

9. Look up and select a Segment ID. I'm picking 200 to correspond with the earlier accounting selection.

10. Click **Insert.**

11. Click **Process** on the menu bar.

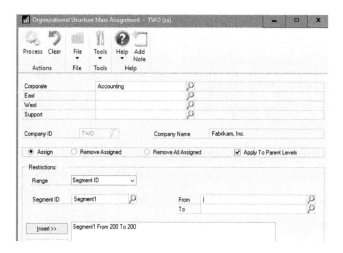

Next, we'll assign these items to users.

1. Select **Administration>Setup>System>Users**.
2. Select a user.
3. Click the organization chart icon next to the user ID.
4. Next to an entity, select a level.
5. Click **Insert**.

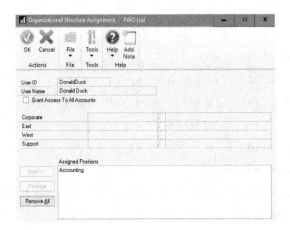

6. Optionally select **Grant Access to All Accounts** to not apply any limits to user.

Finally, activate Account Level Security.

1. Navigate to **Administration>Setup>Company>Company**.
2. Check the box next to **Account Security**.

Account Level Security will affect all users. Do not activate **Account Security** unless **Account Setup** and **Organizational Security** have been properly configured. If these setups have not been completed and Account Security is activated, access will be denied to all accounts in the chart and it will appear that the chart has been deleted. Deactivating account security restores access.

Field Level Security

Field Level Security is used in GP to restrict access to specific items in a window. For example, it can be used to require a password to enter data into a specific field. Field level security is more of a security development tool. For this reason, auditors will typically treat field level security as a mitigating control and want to test the effectiveness of the setup. Since there is a lot of flexibility in field level security, we'll cover the basics to get things started.

There are 10 different types, or variations, that can be applied with field level security. The types are:

- **Password Before** – A user must enter a password before entering data into a field.
- **Password After** – A user must enter a password to exit a specified field. An incorrect password will result in any changes not being saved.
- **Warning Before** – A warning is displayed before a user enters data into a protected field.
- **Lock Field** – The field cannot be used or changed.
- **Disable Field** – The field will be displayed but data cannot be entered or changed.
- **Password Window** – The user will have to enter a password before the window is displayed.
- **Disable Window** – The window cannot be used unless the system administrator password is entered.
- **Password Form** – A password must be entered before any of the windows on a form can be accessed.

- **Disable Form** – The system administrator password must be entered to access the form.

Field level security passwords are functional passwords set in field level security.

 In GP, a form is a container that holds windows. For example, the **Sales Transaction Entry** form contains the **Sales Transaction Entry** window, the **Sales Payment Terms** Window, and the **Scroll: Line Scroll** window.

A Security ID is the identifier for a specific field level security setting. Password protecting a field is a common field level security event so we'll use that as an example. Let's add another layer of security to the security master switch in GP. To create this security ID:

1. Navigate to **Administration>Setup>System>Field Level Security**.
2. Click **Add** at the bottom.
3. Enter a **Security ID** like **Sec Mastr Pass**.
4. Enter a **Description**. This is required. Use *Security Master Password Lock*.
5. On the left click **Microsoft Dynamics GP**.
6. On the right, scroll down and pick **Microsoft Dynamics GP**.

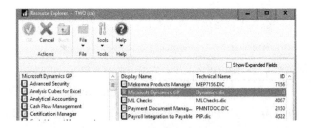

7. On the right, double click **Company** then **Company Setup**.

8. Click **Main: Company Setup**.

9. Click **Use Security**.

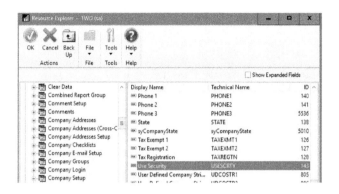

10. Set **Security Mode** to **Password Before**.

11. In **Password ID** key *Sec Master Pass*.

12. Click **Add** to add the password.

13. Enter a Description like: ***Enter the secret password***. The description is often used as a prompt that the user will see.

14. Enter a password.

15. Click **Save** and close the Password Maintenance window.

16. Click **Save** and close the Field Level Security Maintenance window.

119

Next, assign the new security ID to users and companies.

1. Navigate to **Administration>Setup>System>Field Level Security** to open the Field Level Security window.
2. Select the **Sec Mastr Pass** security ID.
3. Check the box next to at least one user.
4. Ensure that the box is checked next to at least one company.
5. Click **Apply**.

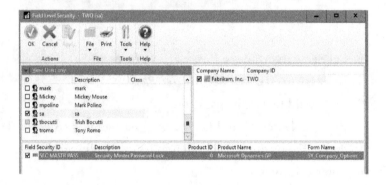

Now, when changing the **Security** box on the **Company Setup** window, Dynamics GP will ask for the field level security password.

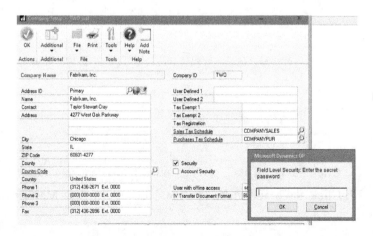

Keep in mind that since these are also functional passwords, one password per function, consequently, multiple users may know the field level security password.

GP Power Tools is a paid add on from Winthrop DC, and one feature of GP Power Tools is the addition of deny based security for Dynamics GP. Deny based security can be used to further restrict access for specific users, even when the user's role would have allowed access.

GL Audit Numbering

GP automatically assigns audit numbers to assist with tracing transactions from subledgers through the general ledger. These are managed via **Administration>Setup>Company>Audit Trail Codes.** Typically, GL Audit Numbering doesn't require any intervention from administrators or users.

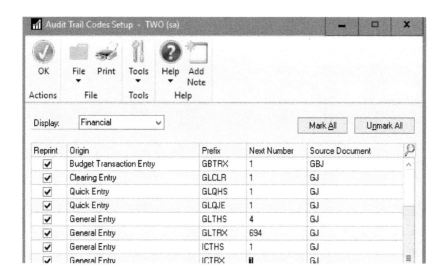

GL Posting Numbers

Consecutive numbering of journal entries without gaps can be an audit or regulatory requirement in many scenarios. GP automatically numbers journal entries, but it is possible to have gaps if entries are deleted prior to posting. GP also reuses journal entry numbers with recurring entries so JE numbers aren't always unique. It is possible to uniquely number each transaction without gaps using the **Posting Numbers** feature in GP. If posting numbers are used, each fiscal year or fiscal period has its own sequence, usually beginning with 1.

To setup posting numbers:

1. Navigate to **Setup>Company>Company>Options**.
2. Check the box next to **Enable Posting Numbers in General Ledger.**
3. This activates a box below marked **Display Posting Numbers per:** with choices for **Year** and **Period.** Select year or period to display posting numbers per fiscal year or fiscal period.

4. An expansion button lights up allowing users to see the next number.

GL inquiries and reports now show the posting number as well as the journal entry number.

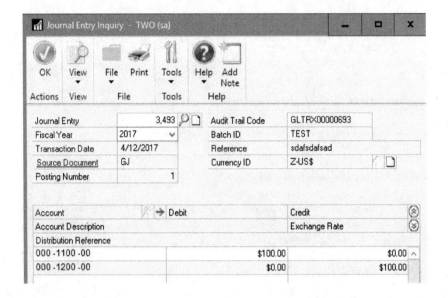

Activity Tracking

Dynamics GP provides an activity tracking option designed to provide some basic tracking information. Users will sometimes try to use this as an audit trail solution. That is the road to disappointment. Activity tracking shows that activity occurred, but it doesn't show what the activity was. For example, Activity Tracking will show that a vendor was changed, and by whom, but not what change was made.

Occasionally, it can still be useful for requests like tracking when users log in and out.

To setup activity tracking:

1. Select **Administration>Setup>System>Activity Tracking**.
2. Select **Login/Logout Tracking** next to **Activity Type**.

3. Mark the **Track** box next to **Successful Attempts to Log In** and **Successful Attempts to Log Out.**

4. Select a user.

5. Check the **Activate** box next to the company or companies to track.

6. Click **OK**

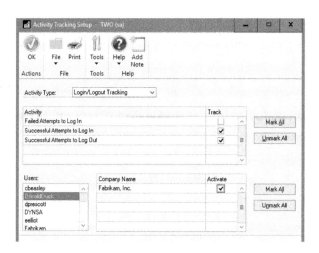

Logged activities can be viewed with inquiry at **Administration>Inquiry>System>Activity Tracking** or on report from **Administration>Report>General>Activity Tracking Detail**.

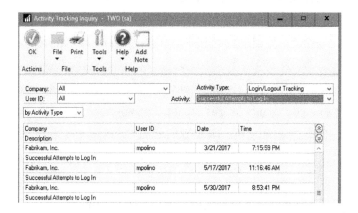

Audit Trail from Fastpath provides real, robust audit trails for GP. Tracking is done at the SQL level and can track changes made via GP, SQL Server Management Studio, third party applications, or any other method. Audit trail records always include the table, record id, original value, new value, date, time, and user who made the change.

User Who Posted

For journal entries and certain other types of transactions, GP records the user ID of the user who posted the transaction. Typically, this information can be viewed via a SmartList.

To view the user who posted for a GL transaction:

1. Select the **Dynamics GP** menu and **SmartLists**.
2. Click the + next to **Financial** to expand the selection.
3. Click **Account Transactions**.
4. Click **Columns** in the menu at the top.
5. Click **Add**.
6. Scroll down and select **User Who Posted**.
7. Click **OK**.
8. Scroll to the right to view the user who posted the transaction.

For journal entries that don't originate in the general ledger and post through the ledger, this user is a pass through from the subledger. Not all subledgers track the user who posted at the origin.

Workflow

Dynamics GP includes a built-in set of workflows. Commonly called Workflow 2.0, these workflows replaced previous SharePoint-based workflows starting with GP 2013 R2. Workflows in GP route transactions for approval or additional tasks based on workflow specifics. GP's workflows were initially approval workflows. Though they now also support tasks, approvals are still the primary use for GP's workflows.

GP supports 15 workflows by default. The out-of-the-box workflows are:

1. General Ledger Batch Approval.
2. Receivables Batch Approval.
3. Payables Batch Approval.
4. Payables Transaction Approval.
5. Purchase Requisition Approval.
6. Purchase Order Approval.
7. Vendor Approval.
8. Employee Profile Approval.
9. Employee Skills Approval.
10. Direct Deposit Approval.
11. Payroll Timecard Approval.
12. W4 Approval.
13. Project Expense Approval.
14. Project Timesheet Approval.
15. SmartList Designer View Approval.

Each workflow can be customized to an extent with specific criteria, email messages, and other details, but only one version of each workflow can be active at a time.

Workflow notifications can be displayed on the GP Home screen and sent via email. Approvals can be made inside of GP or via email through web services. Activities with workflows attached do not complete in GP until the workflow is completed. For example, a requisition cannot be transferred to a purchase order until the requisition workflows approvals are complete.

GP Workflow requires some setup to prepare this feature for use. Since that is a one-time process that can be fairly involved, we won't cover that here, but we highly recommend Ian Grieve's book *Microsoft Dynamics GP Workflow 2.0 Second Edition*. It's available from Amazon at **http://amzn.to/2rvHuRK** .

Workflows are often used as mitigating or compensating controls. For example, if access to create vendors and enter AP vouchers can't be adequately segregated via security, using a vendor approval workflow with an independent review and approval, provides additional control over vendor creation.

Since workflows are not a primary security feature and since GP workflows can get very involved, we will only scratch the surface of what workflows can do using a simple vendor workflow as an example. In this example, a single approval is required to create or make changes to a vendor. To create a vendor workflow:

1. In Dynamics GP select
   Administration>Company>Workflow>Workflow Maintenance.
2. Select **Vendor Approval** in the left pane.
3. Click the lookup button on the right in the box marked **Managers** to add users who can manage this workflow.

 Managers can make any changes to workflow, including adjusting approval limits. Workflow managers should be carefully controlled.

4. Enter the name or Active Directory ID of the user and click the binoculars to search AD for that user.
5. Click **Add** to add the user to **Selected Users**.

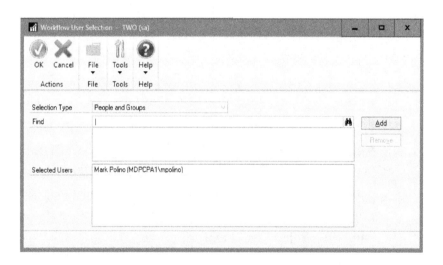

6. Click **OK.**

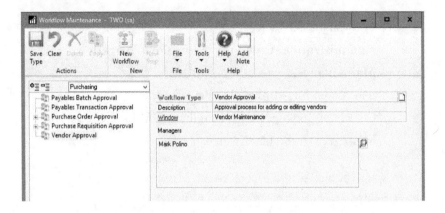

7. Highlight **Vendor Approval** in the left pane and click **New Workflow**.

8. Name the workflow, **Vendor Approve.**

The workflow needs to be saved before individual steps can be added and it needs to be marked as active before it can take effect. We'll setup the rest of the workflow and come back to add steps.

9. In the **Options** section, click the box next to **Send notifications for completed actions.**

10. Click the expansion button, represented by the blue arrow, to open the **Workflow Email Notification Maintenance** window. Checking the box next to an item will notify the originator as the workflow progresses. Check **Submit, Approve, Reject** and **Final Approve.** This will send the originator an email for each of these items.

11. Based on setup, the email message should default. If it does not, the lookup button can be used to select or change the related email message.

12. The **Send carbon copy to** boxes can be used to send notifications to someone other than the originator.

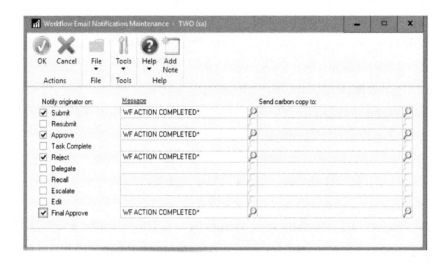

13. The remaining options are:

    a. **Allow approver to delegate tasks** – allows the
       approver to delegate tasks to another approver.

    b. **Allow originator to be an approver** – an originator
       may approve their own workflows. This is not
       recommended for production. However, it is
       extremely useful for testing workflows. Check this
       box for testing, but make sure to uncheck it once
       testing is complete.

    c. **Always require at least one approver** – Even if a
       step does not require approval, require at least one
       approval for this workflow. Essentially, this is a
       safeguard to ensure that steps aren't designed to avoid
       approval.

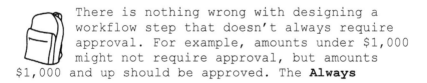

There is nothing wrong with designing a
workflow step that doesn't always require
approval. For example, amounts under $1,000
might not require approval, but amounts
$1,000 and up should be approved. The **Always**

require at least one approver option is helpful for ensuring that complex workflows don't accidently avoid approval.

14. **Use alternate final approver** – provides an alternate final approver for this workflow.

15. Select one of the items in the **When a task is overdue** section. This section defines what happens when a workflow task exceeds the timeline for approval. The options are:

    a. **Take no action** – The workflow step remains open until approved, rejected, or recalled.

    b. **Escalate to next approver** – The workflow moves to the next approver.

    c. **Escalate to** – The workflow moves to the user selected in the box.

    d. **Automatically reject the overdue task** – Automatically process a rejection for the task.

16. Select **Save Workflow**.

Now it's time to go back and add in one or more steps. To do this:

1. Select the **Vendor Approve** workflow that was just created.
2. Click **New Step** to create a step.
3. Name the step *Approval.*
4. Set **Step Type** to **Approval.**
5. Select **Action is always required for this step**.

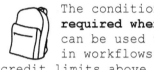

The condition choice: **Action is only required when the following condition is met** can be used to create conditions or branches in workflows. For example, vendors with credit limits above a certain amount could be routed differently for approval. Multiple steps and sub-steps are available as part of the approval conditions. This is a very powerful feature and we encourage users to learn more about workflow conditions.

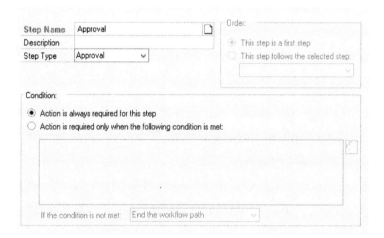

6. Click the lookup button next to **Assign to** and enter an Active Directory user.
7. Use the binocular icon to validate the AD user and click **Add** to add the user.
8. Click **OK.**

133

Workflow is not restricted to Active Directory users; Active Directory groups can also be used. Using groups can make management much easier. As employees come and go, and users change, the groups can stay constant in workflow, but the members of the groups can change in Active Directory.

9. Set the **Time Limit** and optionally check the **Apply Workflow Calendar** box. This time limit is used to determine when a task is overdue to activate the overdue options selected in the workflow setup. The workflow calendar is created in setup and is used to adjust for work days and periods. For example, based on the workflow calendar, a workflow created on a Friday afternoon with a 12-hour time limit would stop counting at 5pm on Friday and resume the time limit at 9am on Monday. This way approvals don't expire during non-work hours.

10. Check the box next to **Send Message** to select a message for the approver. This message may default if a default has been setup.

11. Optionally check the **Include Document Attachments documents** to forward any attached documents as part of the approval process.

12. Select a **Completion policy**. The options are:

    a. **Only one response needed** – only one approver must approve.

    b. **Majority must approve** – with multiple approvers, a majority must approve.

    c. **All must approve** – all assigned users must approve.

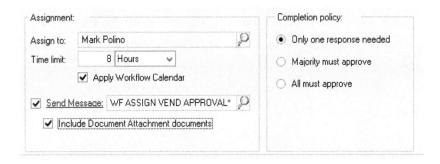

13. Click **Save Step**. This process can be repeated to add multiple steps to a process. The **Order** box in the upper right can be used to identify a step as the first step or as a follow-on step in the process.

Finally, a workflow must be activated. Only one workflow can be active for each category. This allows the creation of a replacement workflow while a primary workflow is still active. To activate a workflow:

1. Select the **Vendor Approve** workflow created earlier.
2. Check the box next to **Active**.
3. Click **Save Workflow**.

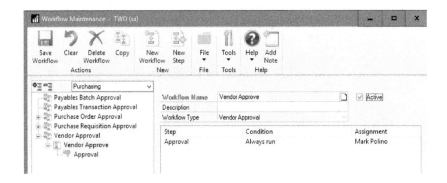

Once a workflow is active, buttons will appear on the transaction to submit a workflow. Users can approve workflows via links in approval emails, buttons on the transaction, or buttons on navigation lists. The approval options available may depend on the user's GP license level.

To view workflow history, find the related item and pick **Workflow History**.

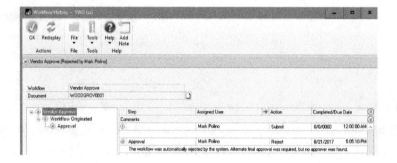

We've just scratched the surface of what can be done with workflow in Dynamics GP. Workflow is one of the most useful options for mitigating controls.

{6}

ADDITIONAL CONTROL CONSIDERATIONS

- Access Review and Certification
- Monitoring

This chapter addresses other control items that weren't previously covered or need some extra emphasis. Backup and restore processes and security reporting are important monitoring activities. Security review is often overlooked and a key piece of access review and certification. We'll also tackle a couple of leftovers.

Principles

In addition to all the things we've looked at, there are a few other control items that are important, and we want to make sure we cover them.

Backup and Restore

A key, basic control is backing up and restoring ERP data. If everything goes wrong, being able to restore data is a last-ditch control. It's tough to deliver financial statements if system information is known to be wrong, and it's almost impossible if there's no information in the system.

In an ERP system maintained on premise, the responsibility for backing up, validating, and restoring information usually falls on the company's IT staff. However, the responsibility for the information contained within the ERP system belongs to the accounting team. This shared responsibility means that accounting can't simply defer responsibility and assume the ERP system is being backed up. There must also be a process to test restoring backed up information on a regular basis.

Ideally, the backup and restore process should be part of a larger, documented disaster recovery plan that includes the company's risk tolerance for lost data and downtime. The key point is testing the recovery. For many companies, a simple test of the recovery process is to periodically restore a backup of production to a test or development environment.

These test and dev environments are usually refreshed at some type of interval, and restoring them from a scheduled backup is one way of validating the backup and restore process. Note, the restore shouldn't be done from backups made specifically for restoring to test, but from a regularly scheduled backup.

In an online model, the responsibility for backup and restore usually rests with the provider. Again, though, there is a shared responsibility to ensure the backup and restore process works as designed. It is important that the process, timing, and any limitations are completely understood. The process of restoring from a backup to a test environment also works well in an online model to ensure that backups can be restored.

Security Reviews

Security reviews are another important control consideration. Security reviews are just that – a review of many of the security controls we've already looked at. Security reviews include things like periodic reviews for orphaned users, access reviews, and segregation of duties monitoring. For a security review to be effective, issues and anomalies need to be investigated and either fixed or documented. For a security review to have taken place, there needs to be evidence, typically in the form of a report and a signature, electronic or physical. Without evidence that a review has been done, auditors are forced to conclude that the review did not occur.

Security Reports

Security reviews rely primarily on security reporting. These can be traditional reports, alerts, ad hoc reports, etc. Security reports can be delivered on a schedule or run manually; again, the key is providing evidence of reviews.

Customizations and Modifications

Instead of doing the hard work of setting security, some companies try to extensively customize Dynamics GP to limit what users can do. Typically, this is the wrong approach. Extensive customization reduces flexibility and makes it difficult to adjust to changing business processes. It can also make it harder to audit GP since customizations are not standard by definition and would require additional testing by auditors.

Third Party Applications

Security considerations should also not be confined to a single application. Typically, GP is part of an ecosystem of products that can include applications like a report writer (Management Reporter, Jet Reports, etc.), integration tool (SmartConnect or Scribe), customer relationship management (Microsoft CRM or Salesforce.com), etc.

It's important to understand that ERP security is not limited to just Dynamics GP, but should include the segregation of duties relationship among related products.

Application

Backup and Restore

Backing up Dynamics GP data is typically performed by I.T. users using tools in SQL Server or via third party SQL tools. For regularly scheduled backups, this is still the preferred option. Backing up via SQL offers greater flexibility in backup types and timing. However, there are options to perform backups inside of Dynamics GP. Backups can be saved to local storage or Microsoft Azure.

To use GP's built-in backup features, the user must be logged into GP as 'sa' or as a user with sysadmin rights in SQL as described earlier in this book.

To perform a local backup:

1. Select **Microsoft Dynamics GP>Maintenance>Backup**.
2. Select the company to backup or select **System Database** to back up the system database (typically Dynamics).
3. Select **Use local storage**.
4. Click the folder icon to select a location for backup.
5. Optionally select the **Use compression box** to compress the backup.
6. Click **OK** to start the backup.

Backing up to Azure requires some additional work and is especially straightforward. IT assistance here may be required. A useful resource to get the setup right is the *Microsoft Dynamics GP 2013 R2 - Backup and Restore in Microsoft Azure* blog post found at: **https://community.dynamics.com/gp/b/dynamicsgp/archive/2014/0 6/04/microsoft-dynamics-gp-2013-r2-backup-and-restore-in-microsoft-azure.**

First, a storage location needs to be setup. We've got a very simplistic set of instructions, but there are a lot of options, so we recommend getting some expertise. Assuming there is already a working Azure environment:

1. In the Azure portal, select **More services>Storage>Storage accounts >Add**.
2. Name the storage account.
3. Set **Account kind** to **General Storage**.
4. Optionally enable encryption and require secure transfer.
5. Create or add this to a resource group.
6. Click **Create**.

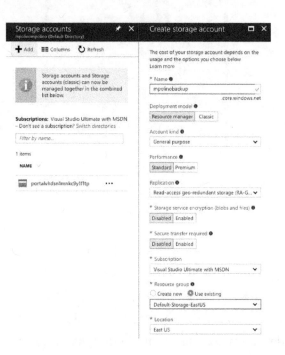

This action takes anywhere from a few seconds, to a minute or two to complete. Now that storage has been created, we need a blob container. To setup a blob container:

1. Refresh the **Storage accounts** page to see the new storage location.
2. Click the new storage location to open it.
3. Navigate to **Blob Service>Containers.**
4. Click **+ Container** to add a new container.
5. Name the container. At this point, it must be all lower case.
6. Leave **Access** set to **Private.**
7. Click **OK**.
8. Click the blob storage account and pick **Access Keys**. Copy and save the key to paste into GP. The **Storage account name** from this window is also required for GP.

9. Click **Containers** to return to the blob.
10. Click the container name to open the container and pick **Properties**.
11. Copy and paste the URL from properties for later use in GP.

1. Select **Microsoft Dynamics GP>Maintenance>Backup**.
2. Pick **Use Microsoft Azure Storage**.
3. Copy the **Storage account** name from Azure.
4. Copy the value from **key1** in Azure to **Access Key** in GP.
5. Copy the URL from the Azure blob container to **URL to container.**

6. Click **Verify** to validate that GP can connect to the Azure storage container. If the connection does not verify, validate the Azure elements. Another troubleshooting option is to regenerate the keys with the circular arrow icons and enter the new keys in GP.

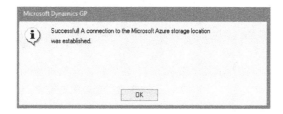

7. Click **OK** to save and start a backup. There is no way to save the Azure information without starting a backup. Note that Azure backups will normally take longer than on-premise backups.

Restoring data is similar with the caveat that a company can't be restored if it is open. To restore a locally backed up GP database:

1. Select **Microsoft Dynamics GP>Maintenance>Restore.**
2. Select the company to restore or select **System Database** to restore the system database (typically Dynamics).
3. Select **Use local storage**.
4. Click the folder icon to select a file to restore.
5. Click **OK** to start the restore.

Restoring from Azure is also like the Azure backup process. To restore from an Azure backup:

1. Select **Microsoft Dynamics GP>Maintenance>Restore.**
2. Select the company to restore or select **System Database** to restore the system database (typically Dynamics).
3. Select **Use Microsoft Azure storage.**
4. For the first restore, reenter the Azure Storage account name, Access Key, and URL to container. Subsequent restores will retain the Azure information.
5. Click **Verify Account.**
6. Enter or verify the file to be restored.
7. Click **OK** to restore the company.

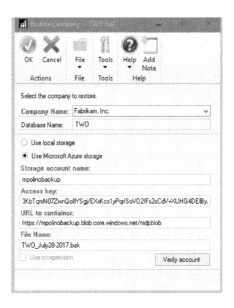

Security Reviews and Reporting

We've already looked at some core GP reports. These reports along with SmartLists form the backbone of what's available for security reviews in Dynamics GP. Some common reports include:

- Security Task Setup
- Security Role Setup
- Security Role Assignment
- Security Task Assignment
- User Security
- Unassigned Security Operations
- Alternate/Modified Forms and Reports
- Company Access
- Company Settings
- Posting Settings

There are no default SmartLists for security information, but a SmartList could be built using SmartList designer for some additional security reporting. Additionally, there are no included SSRS reports related to security in GP.

Some critical items, like segregation of duties, can be difficult and time-consuming to review with GP reports. Also, we've covered sign-off for reviews at length in the principles section, but GP doesn't provide a mechanism for electronic signatures on reports. This issue is something that will need to be addressed with a policy that could include physical reviews and signatures, or a third-party option like Assure from Fastpath.

 Fastpath Assure includes a prebuilt, customizable segregation of duties rule set combined with SoD conflict analysis to make analyzing segregations of duties much easier. Additionally, Assure's access review reporting can provide improved reporting and insights into GP's security setup. Finally, Assure facilitates electronic signatures for security reviews, making it easy to provide evidence of ongoing reviews.

{7}

AUDITING DYNAMICS GP

- Monitoring

Auditing is all about monitoring and validating that controls are working properly. We took a different approach in this chapter, but we think it's important.

Principles

While this book is primarily about setting up and managing security in Dynamics GP, auditing is an important part of validating that security and controls are working as designed.

Auditing

We won't spend much time on auditing principles. So much has been written about auditing principles that we could never recap it all in this book. We're using the term auditing a bit generically here, in that the audit in question could be an external audit that is focused on the integrity of financial statements, it could be an internal audit geared toward process improvement or segregation of duties, or something as simple as monitoring the effectiveness of specific controls.

We suspect that readers who are more audit-focused might skip over other chapters and come directly here. For that reason, we've built in some overlap with items covered in other chapters, but we think it's helpful to have these items grouped together in a single chapter, even if some basic information is repeated. The application steps may be a little shorter too, as we aren't going quite as deep for these items. Know that many of these items are covered in greater depth throughout the book. Finally, this isn't an exhaustive list of audit tools and options, but we tried to hit the big stuff.

Application

Activity Tracking

Activity Tracking is a logging feature in GP that can track basic information on changes. It is often referenced incorrectly as a solution to auditing changes in GP. In the real world, activity tracking is woefully inadequate as an actual audit trail. Activity tracking shows that a record was changed, and by whom. It does not track, capture, or show actual changes to the record.

If activity tracking is turned on, activity logs are available in GP via:

- **Administration>Inquiry>System>Activity Tracking**
- **Administration>Reports>System>General**

Microsoft no longer offers an audit trail solution for Dynamics GP. They recommend using third party solutions like Fastpath's Audit Trail.

Audit Trail from Fastpath provides a true audit trail solution that tracks changes at the database level, regardless of the tool used to make the change. Audit Trail reporting includes the record that was changed, the value before and after the change, the user, and the date and time of the change.

Last User, User Who Posted & Approvals

GP's general ledger includes information on the last user of a transaction, the user who posted, and the user who approved, if approvals were activated. Transactions originating in a subledger are identifiable from those originating in the GL using the Source Document field.

The Last User field tends to be unreliable for a couple of reasons. First, transactions that originate in the subledger typically don't populate the last user, and if they do, it's often populated with the posting user id. Second, if the posting user opens a journal entry to review it prior to posting, GP updates the last user with their ID.

Last user, user who posted, and source document (to identify journal entries that originate in the general ledger) are available to be added to a SmartList.

To add these and run a SmartList:

1. Select **Microsoft Dynamics GP>SmartList>Financial>Account Transactions**.
2. Click **Columns>Add**.
3. Scroll down and, while holding the Control key, select **Last User, Source Document,** and **User Who Posted**.

4. Click **OK**.

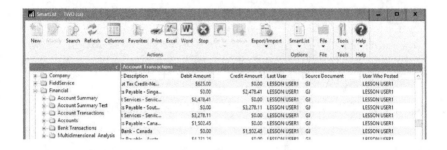

Oddly, approval user id (APRVLUSERID) and approval date (APPRVLDT) are not available to select in a SmartList, even though they are present in the table. These two fields can be added via SmartList builder (more work than we can delve into here) or by directly querying the GL20000 (Open Year) or GL30000 (Historical Years) tables. If approvals are used for subledger transactions, approvals will be tracked in the related open or history tables.

Workflow approvals can be seen on individual transactions with workflow assigned using the **View History** button.

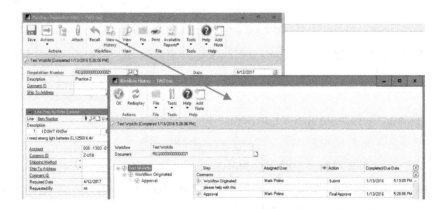

Security Reporting

GP offers a set of security reports to help with understanding and documenting security. These reports are found via **Administration>Reports>System>Security** and include:

- **Security Task Setup** – Security operations assigned to each task.
- **Security Role Setup** – Security tasks assigned to each role.
- **Security Role Assignment** – Users assigned to each security role.
- **Security Task Assignment** – Users associated with each security task.
- **User Security** – Users, their assigned role and associated task.
- **Unassigned Security Operations** – A list of security operations not assigned to any task.
- **Alternate/Modified Forms and Reports** – Report on the alternate/modified status of windows and reports.

Note, there is not an easy way to export these reports to Excel. GP doesn't include security reporting in SmartLists or refreshable Excel reports.

Common Reports for Audit

Common finance reports for audit include:

- Trial Balance (**Financial>Reports>Trial Balance>Summary**)

153

- Payables Historical Aged Trial Balance
  (**Purchasing>Reports>Trial Balance>Historical Aged Trial Balance**)
- Receivables Historical Aged Trial Balance
  (**Sales>Reports>Trial Balance>Historical Aged Trial Balance)**
- Historical Inventory Aged Trial Balance
  (**Inventory>Reports>Activity>Historical IV Trial Balance**)
- Received not Invoiced (Accrued Purchases)
  (**Purchasing>Reports>Analysis>Received not Invoiced**)

 The historical trial balances for AP, AR and Inventory are difficult to export to Excel in a usable format. Mark Polino has Excel-based versions of these reports built on the stored procedures provided by Microsoft as part of Dynamics GP. The Excel reports are available for sale at **http://mpolino.com/gp/historical-excel-reporting/**.

Fastpath Tools

Fastpath **Assure** provides a comprehensive audit solution to automate risk management and Sarbanes-Oxley compliance for Dynamics GP. This includes segregation of duties analysis using an easily customizable, out-of-the-box ruleset to quickly analyze security conflicts within and across roles. Also included is additional security analysis, simple sign-off for mitigations, and scheduled report delivery.

Fastpath's **Audit Trail** provides continuous monitoring in the form of true change tracking and reporting for Dynamics GP. **Config AD** delivers single sign-on functionality with Active Directory. Finally,

Identity Manager from Fastpath delivers workflow-based provisioning for GP users with SoD conflict analysis, including editing and terminating GP, along with user, role, and global permission level effective dates.

SUMMARY

Security is an important consideration in any financial system and Dynamics GP is no exception. GP provides a wealth of security options and tools to help companies establish a secure control environment. In addition to GP's built-in tools, additional applications, like Fastpath Assure, Audit Trail and Config AD, provide an important supplement to Dynamics GP's governance, risk, and compliance capabilities.

Ultimately, no software can perfectly secure a working environment. Companies are responsible for implementing a complete control environment including appropriate controls, segregation of duties, and taking a risk-based approach to the process.

In this book, we've tried to highlight the principles underlying good security and explain how to apply those principles to a Dynamics GP environment. This book can't address every situation, but we hope that we've helped with the most common and relevant issues. GP's documentation provides a wealth of information to address scenarios that go beyond this book. Additionally, Fastpath provides a host of tools designed to help companies address their security, audit, and compliance needs in Dynamics GP.

EDITION NOTE

Microsoft Dynamics GP has a long history of regular releases, with both major releases and significant interim updates. This can be a problem for GP books. Without regular updates, book content grows stale. Is a book written for GP in 2010 still relevant to GP 2016?

To ensure relevance, we're making a commitment to update this book with each major GP release. Our editions are numbered in conjunction with GP's numbering system. This edition is 2016 to correspond with the current release of GP. If we must make a significant change in the book prior to the next GP release, we'll number the new release 2016 Mk1. The Mk1 fits nicely with the field manual theme and indicates a book change, not a GP change.

Some releases may only have a few security related changes, while others could see significant rework. GP continues to add additional security features, and with a topic as important as security and audit, we feel it's important to keep up to date.

You can find additional information at:
https://www.gofastpath.com/gpbook.

INDEX